Academic Discourse

D1290314

Academic Discourse

*Linguistic Misunderstanding and
Professorial Power*

Pierre Bourdieu, Jean-Claude Passeron and
Monique de Saint Martin,
with contributions by Christian Baudelot
and Guy Vincent

Translated by Richard Teese

Stanford University Press
Stanford, California

Stanford University Press
Stanford, California
© 1965 Mouton et Cie as *Rapport Pédagogique et
    Communication*
English translation and Preface © 1994 Polity
    Press in association with Blackwell Publishers Ltd
Originating publisher of English edition: Polity
    Press, Cambridge
First published in the U.S.A. by
    Stanford University Press
Printed in Great Britain
Paper ISBN 0-8047-2688-4
Cloth ISBN 0-8047-2333-8
This book is printed on acid-free paper.

Contents

Preface to the English Language Edition

Academic Discourse is a translation of a work which originally appeared in French in 1965 under the title *Rapport pédagogique et communication*. Apart from the change of title and the addition of a glossary compiled by the translator, the text has not been altered or revised. The study is based on research that was carried out in French universities in the early 1960s. But the main findings and central arguments of the study – concerning, above all, the role of language and linguistic misunderstanding in the educational process – retain their significance today.

Glossary

---

agrégation   University examination (*concours*) qualifying the candidate to teach in a *lycée* or in certain university faculties.

année propédeutique   Between 1948 and 1966 there existed a preliminary year in French universities designed to prepare students for university study and to exclude students considered unfit. In the text, this is translated 'preliminary year'.

B.U.S.   University Bureau of Statistics & School and Vocational Guidance.

baccalauréat   Examination ending academic secondary schooling and permitting entry to higher education. Part I was administered at the end of 11th grade (and as a condition for entry to the 12th grade), Part II at the end of the 12th grade.

bachelier   Person who has obtained the *baccalauréat*.

C.A.P.E.S.   *Certificat d'aptitude pédagogique à l'enseignement secondaire* – Certificate of Secondary Teaching Proficiency, qualifying the holder to teach in secondary schools.

cagneux (khâgneux)   Students in post-secondary classes of the major *lycées*, studying for admission to the *grandes écoles*. In the text, these are referred to as 'preparatory students'.

classes préparatoires   *Classes préparatoires aux grandes écoles* – post-secondary classes in the major *lycées* in which students prepare over two years for the entrance examinations to the *grandes écoles*.

collège Public secondary school differing, historically, from the *lycée* by its connection with a municipality (rather than directly with the state). After successive reforms (1959–75), the term *collège* is now applied to four-year junior secondary schools, leading to the *lycée* or senior secondary school.

cours secondaires Classes in secondary education organized by a municipality which lacked a *lycée* or *collège*.

École normale supérieure Founded in 1794, an elite tertiary institution with various sections, training teachers for all branches of secondary education. Students follow university lectures as well as classes given by ENS staff.

examen probatoire Name given to Part I of the *baccalauréat* when this became an internal examination.

grandes écoles Higher professional schools, selective in terms of intake, often superior to universities in prestige, and offering access to elite positions in government and business.

licence Corresponds to a bachelor's degree and comprises four or five certificates (depending on the subject) obtained after exams.

lycée Academic secondary school which, in the early 1960s, offered the whole seven years of secondary education.

petit séminaire Secondary school run by the Catholic Church.

sixième The first grade in a *lycée* or *collège*. In France, year-levels of secondary education are enumerated from the *sixième* to the *première* and *classe terminale*, in descending order.

Introduction: Language and Relationship to Language in the Teaching Situation

Pierre Bourdieu
Jean-Claude Passeron

The ideal lecture theatre is vast, truly vast. *It is a very sombre, very old amphitheatre, and very uncomfortable. The professor is lodged in his chair, which is raised high enough so that everyone can see him; there is no question that he might get down and pester you. You can hear him quite well, because he doesn't move. Only his mouth moves.*

Preferably he has white hair, a stiff neck and a Protestant air about him. There are a great many students, and each is perfectly anonymous.

To reach the amphitheatre, you have to climb some stairs, and then, with the leather-lined doors closed behind, the silence is absolute, every sound stifled; the walls rise very high, daubed with rough paintings in half-tones in which the moving silhouettes of various monsters can be detected. Everything adds to the impression of being in another world. So one works religiously.

(History student, female, aged 25, Paris)

To Henrietta and Edwin DODGSON

                    Ch{rist} Ch{urch} Oxford, 31 January 1855.

My dear Henrietta,
My dear Edwin,

(. . .) *My one pupil has begun his work with me, and I will give you a description of how the lecture is conducted. It is the most important point, you know, that the tutor should be dignified and at a distance from the pupil, and that the pupil should be as much as possible degraded. Otherwise, you know, they are not humble enough.*

So I sit at the further end of the room: outside the door (which is shut) sits the scout; outside the outer door (also shut) sits the sub-scout; half-way downstairs sits the sub-sub-scout; and down in the yard sits the pupil.

The questions are shouted from one to the other, and the answers come back in the same way – it is rather confusing till you are well used to it. The lecture goes on something like this:

Tutor: What is twice three?
Scout: What's a rice-tree?
Sub-scout: When is ice free?
Sub-sub-scout: What's a nice fee?
Pupil (timidly): *Half a guinea!*
Sub-sub-scout: Can't forge any!
Sub-scout: Ho for jinny!
Scout: Don't be a ninny!
Tutor (looking offended, tries another question): *Divide a hundred by twelve!*
Scout: Provide wonderful bells!
Sub-scout: Go ride under it yourself!
Sub-sub-scout: Deride the dunderheaded elf!
Pupil (surprised): *Who do you mean?*
Sub-sub-scout: Doings between.
Sub-scout: Blue is the screen!
Scout: Soup-tureen!

And so the lecture proceeds. Such is life.

Your most affectionate brother,
Charles L. Dodgson

                    (Lewis Carroll, *Letters to his Child-Friends*)

Words must often play the part of these badly trained scouts, sub-scouts and sub-sub-scouts if the teaching staff of our universities are not trained to manage the sound effects of the communication that passes between them and their students. Destined to dazzle rather than to enlighten, the academic livery of the word fulfils the eminent function of keeping the pupil at a distance. *E longinquo reverentia*: respectful distance and respect through distance.

Modern societies claim to have transformed teaching into a highly efficient form of communication, based on specialized methods and techniques. The effectiveness of contemporary teaching practice should therefore be measurable by the amount of information which students actually receive.[1] But examinations, special tests, interviews and direct questioning all show that an unacceptably high loss of information occurs in the way teaching is currently conducted in French universities, at least in faculties of arts.

Academics and students agree that there is a crisis in education. But they have failed to get to its roots, and have fallen into endless recriminations. The most common diagnoses of our system are simply rationalizations which make its failings more bearable by handing us convenient slogans. Surely we need to question the underlying social and political functions of a teaching relationship which so often fails, yet has not provoked a revolt, and which is so often attacked, but only ritualistically or ideologically.

No one can doubt that the declining quality of teaching in French universities today owes a great deal to enormous physical and resource problems. But the attitudes of academics and students are also implicated. There can be no prospect of achieving real change until it is recognized that teaching is a system. It will continue to operate as a system (even badly) only so long as the functional links between student and teacher attitudes and the material and institutional conditions underpinning them are maintained. If higher education is so resistant to change, perhaps this is because visible tensions and conflicts mask deeper relationships undergirding the system and providing a real degree of security behind the outward signs of frustration. In short, research into the causes of the linguistic misunderstanding which characterizes the teaching relationship must extend to the functions which this failure serves in perpetuating the system. Every effort to transform the system which is not accompanied by an attempt to transform attitudes towards the system (and conversely) is doomed to failure.

Linguistic misunderstanding

Teaching depends for its effectiveness on a variety of inputs, with material conditions in the first rank. The output of an academic system, on the other hand, is determined by the absolute or relative quantity of information transmitted through language. For there are few activities which consist so exclusively as teaching in the manipulation of words. Testing students on the words actually used in lectures shows that it is the nature of university language and how it is applied which are the most critical, but least cited, causes of the breakdown in the teaching relationship. The test results bluntly expose the complacency of those academics who claim that the system has not made dupes of them, but who cling to the traditional language of ideas because it is accepted without opposition.[2]

Many university students are unable to cope with the technical and scholastic demands made on their use of language as students. They cannot define the terms which they hear in lectures or which they themselves use. They are remarkably tolerant of words lifted from the language of ideas but applied inappropriately or irrelevantly, and they accept sloppiness and incorrectness with resigned indifference. The lexis and syntax of examination scripts and essays written during the year offer a still more unchallengeable test of linguistic misunderstanding.[3] Constrained to write in a badly understood and poorly mastered language, many students are condemned to using a *rhetoric of despair* whose logic lies in the reassurance that it offers. Through a kind of incantatory or sacrificial rite, they try to call up and reinstate the tropes, schemas or words which to them distinguish professorial language. Irrationally and irrelevantly, with an obstinacy that we might too easily mistake for servility, they seek to reproduce this discourse in a way which recalls the simplifications, corruptions and logical re-workings that linguists encounter in 'creolized' languages.

Convenient it would be to reject the problem of linguistic misunderstanding as due simply to the use and abuse of philosophical or technical jargon. But our evidence relates to how language is employed by students in philosophy and the human sciences, disciplines whose vocabularies may be most esoteric, but which, at the same time, are more specific than those of other humanities. In these fields, academics, as well as students, are professionally trained in the correct and precise management of specialized vocabularies and in the rigorous linking of ideas. If tolerance of linguistic misunderstanding is so great in these domains, it is likely to be even greater in the teaching of other arts subjects. For in the humanities more broadly, the direct borrowing of a scholastic vocabulary from the current language of ideas does not reduce poor comprehension and mismanagement of language, but only awareness of these problems.

What makes linguistic misunderstanding in the teaching relationship so serious is that it goes beyond the superficialities of jargon to the operation of a *code*. If academics nourished illusions only about the quantity of information that students were capable of learning or retaining, the impact on the teaching relationship would be less serious than the presumption that students know – because they ought to know – the underlying code of the professorial message. Of course, there is no communication without disturbing background effects, and this 'static' is likely to be greatest in the pedagogical communication between the one who knows and the one who is to learn. Indeed, learning implies acquiring both knowledge itself and the code of transmission used to convey a particular body of knowledge. The code cannot be learnt except through a progressively less unskilled decoding of messages. All real apprenticeship, including the more diffuse processes of socialization and acculturation, are governed by this logic. But what distinguishes communication which is pedagogical is the specific role of its technicians in methodically and continuously reducing to a minimum the misunderstanding arising from the use of the code.

Communication can only be regarded as pedagogical when every effort is made to eliminate the faulty 'signals' inherent in an incomplete knowledge of the code and to transmit the code in the most efficient way. The signs of *anomie* in the teaching rationship are apparent when explicit and systematic efforts to reduce communicative failure are rare, and when most students accept linguistic misunderstanding as a necessary evil which the skills of the teacher are not required to address.[4]

To seek to measure the output of pedagogical communication is to agree to judge teaching according to its own standard. Pedagogy loses all meaning unless it reflects the intention to communicate rationally, and thus to completely rationalize the means of communication. Teaching is at its most effective not when it succeeds in transmitting the greatest quantity of information in the shortest time (and at the least cost), but rather when most of the information conveyed by the teacher is actually received. Consequently, the output from the teaching relationship can be measured by the expression 'quantity of information conveyed by A to B / quantity of information received by B from A'; or again, the expression 'quantity of information conveyed by A to B / quantity of information received by A from B'. The student's ability to relay a message back to the teacher (for correction or confirmation) is captured by the second expression, which measures the success of the action of forming ideas and of transforming knowledge more effectively than the first.

However, neither way of measuring the output of pedagogical communication takes account of how external factors influence teaching effectiveness. In reality, the teaching situation is constrained in a variety of ways, including the kinds of pressures which students and academics are placed under during the year and the buildup of fears about the absolute minimum of content that must be covered. It would be a poor strategy in this context to deal with the problem of information loss simply by cutting down on content, as happens in those non-directive teaching practices which claim a high rate of assimilation, but at the cost of a large reduction in the absolute quantity of information which is actually conveyed. To question the effectiveness of pedagogical communication in terms of output brings into focus the problems of teaching which our relationship to academic language has enabled us to avoid. There are, in fact, two systems of contradictory demands that pedagogical communication needs to satisfy, neither of which can be completely sacrificed: first, to maximize the absolute quantity of information conveyed (which implies reducing repetition and redundancy to a minimum); second, to minimize loss of information (which, among other measures, may imply an increase in redundancy). The optimal use of language in teaching requires that we recognize the things that separate communicator from receiver and, in particular, the receiver's knowledge of the codes of communication and the dependence of this knowledge on factors such as social origin and school career.

Any attempt to construct a view of teaching which is governed by a genuinely pedagogical intention will inevitably appear utopian. For even the aim of maximizing the output of communication, not to mention fulfilling the intellectual demands underlying this, goes directly against the traditional relationship to the language of teaching. There is a visible abyss to be crossed between redundancy of a traditional nature, like musical variations on a theme, and redundancy of a rational kind, like conscious and calculated repetition (for example, in the form of the definition), or again between ellipsis by omission and understatement and conciseness guided by the need for economy.[5]

Ethnocentrism of the profession

Similarly, when we try to make teaching more effective by clarifying its goals and the conditions needed to improve its efficiency, we clash with the pedagogical philosophy of academics, whose disdain for the 'elementary' nature of a reflexive pedagogy reflects the superior level of the education system which they occupy. Their rejection of an explicit teaching practice follows from a perception of the student favoured by the professorial craft, one which is armed with all the certitudes and all the blindnesses of cultural ethnocentrism. Defined by their lesser knowledge, students can do nothing which does not confirm the most pessimistic image that the professor, in his most professional capacity, is willing to confess to: they understand nothing; and they reduce the most brilliant theories to logical monstrosities or picturesque oddities, as if their only role in life was to illustrate the vanity of the efforts which the professor squanders on them and which he will continue to squander, despite everything, out of professional conscience, with a disabused lucidity which only redoubles his merit. By definition, the professor teaches as he ought to teach, and the meagre results with which he is rewarded can only reinforce his certainty that the great majority of his students are unworthy of the efforts he bestows upon them.[6] Indeed, the professor is as resigned to his students and their 'natural' incapacities as the 'good colonist' is to the 'natives', for whom he has no higher expectations than that they be just the way they are. Attempts to combat linguistic misunderstanding are widely absent among academics because, for one thing, teaching *naturally* implies poor reception of the best messages by the worst receivers.

Teaching brings together partners distinguished by different degrees of expertise and separated not only by inequalities in the amounts of knowledge they possess, but also by profoundly different intellectual and professional approaches. Neophyte and master will never have the same perception of the task and the whole business of obtaining a qualification, and it is from this that the often observed breach between student expectations and teacher behaviour arises. Academics, for example, will often put the accent in their lectures on the progress of reason or on the method and structure of great works – in short, on *form*. For this is just what gives value and intellectual interest to their work, and confirms its connection with culture. Students, on the other hand, often want content, whether this means the 'emotional' aspect of literary works (in arts and philosophy) or end results which represent the outcome of theory (in the human and natural sciences). Values peculiar to adolescence underlie an expectation of charismatic or traditional teaching, a total teaching that will prepare one for a total place in life. Consciously or unconsciously, the great majority of students (especially in the humanities) cast the professor in the role of 'master of wisdom', or guru, dispenser of rules of life. Encouraged by an education which still frequently claims to impart 'wisdom' and which 'points towards life', in the words of the 'sage masters', these expectations belong to a metaphysical age. They are nearly always dashed, because the academic discourse on life tends to 'neutralize' (in the phenomenological sense) the thing about which it speaks simply by speaking about it, and by speaking about it in the manner and in the place where it speaks.

The 'great teachers' at schools are often those who agree to satisfy this adolescent longing by giving their teaching a charismatic emphasis. If many who leave a mark on our school memories are teachers of philosophy, this is because the *lycée* brings together the most favourable conditions – the age of the pupils, the particular training of the teacher, his place within the school, the programmes, the timetables – and it is these conditions which confer upon the teacher and upon what he teaches the prestige of something above everyday life. Such an encounter, which is characteristic of French education, certainly plays a positive role, if only by encouraging a commitment to the values of an apprenticeship in culture. For similar reasons, this type of teaching relationship seems to extend to the preliminary year in arts faculties.[7] But once this year has been completed, students find it quite disconcerting when they enter the necessarily more technical cycle of the *licence*.[8] Between student and professor, only complicity in mutual misunderstanding can authorize a polemical relationship on the part of each to the values of the other and at the same time an ideological relationship to his own values. With no risk to himself, the protesting student can lay down expectations which would apply in an ideal world, but which would require that he give up his amateurism; while the traditionalist professor can slide from the *right* to demand that his students learn, which all teaching implies, to the *fact* of making this demand when he has withheld from them the means of satisfying it.

Class ethnocentrism

The most hidden spring of professorial *certitudo sui*, the ethnocentrism of class, thus escapes both teacher and student. In secondary and higher education, it is taken for granted that the language of ideas elaborated by the academic and scientific tradition and also the second-order language of allusions and cultural complicities are second nature to intelligent and gifted individuals; or better, that the ability to understand and to manipulate these learned languages – artificial languages, *par excellence* – where we see the natural language of human intelligence at work immediately distinguishes intelligent students from all the rest. It is thanks to this ideology of a profession that academics can vouch for professorial judgements as strictly equitable. But in reality they consecrate cultural privilege. Language is the most active and elusive part of the cultural heritage which each individual owes to his background. This is because language does not reduce, as we often think, to a more or less extensive collection of words. As syntax, it provides us with a system of transposable mental dispositions. These go hand in hand with values which dominate the whole of our experience and, in particular, with a vision of society and of culture. They also involve an original relationship to words, reverential or free, borrowed or familiar, sparing or intemperate.[9]

Academic language is a dead language for the great majority of French people, and is no one's mother tongue, not even that of children of the cultivated classes. As such, it is very unequally distant from the language actually spoken by the different social classes. To decline to offer a rational pedagogy is, in this context, to declare that all students are equal in respect of the demands made by academic language. It is also to be condemned, by the same stroke, to ascribing many inequalities which originate in social organization to differences in natural 'gifts'. Outside school, working-class children have no access to cultural works, so the teaching of culture always anticipates an experience of culture which is missing. The divorce between the language of the family and the language of school only serves to reinforce the feeling that the education system belongs to another world, and that what teachers have to say has nothing to do with daily life because spoken in a language which makes it unreal. The world of the classroom, where 'polished' language is used, contrasts with the world of the family, and even more with the world of the provincial boarding-school (which gathers mainly lower-status children from the countryside). This rift extends across all dimensions of life, from central areas of interest to the very words in which these are discussed; and it can be lived only with a sense of dualism or in a state of resigned submission to being excluded. It is true that this problem arises mostly at the level of secondary education, because working-class students are still rare in university faculties and because, in the current situation, they owe their access to this higher level to a particularly successful adaptation to the language of teaching. The milieu of the university student also seems to provide a secondary linguistic setting which facilitates apprenticeship in the language of ideas.[10] However, any democratization of recruitment to university will need to be matched by a deliberate effort to rationalize techniques of communication. Otherwise the linguistic and cultural misunderstanding which today marks secondary education – where it remains to be researched and tackled methodically – will reach the same acute levels in higher education.

In our search for the causes of the breakdown in the contemporary teaching relationship, we tend to look for factors which can be examined at a very general level and which thus escape any direct and immediate intervention. Perhaps this is what we expect from such a cavalier and totalizing sociology. We often invoke the gap between the generations. We assume, implicitly and gratuitously, that the cultural distance which supposedly sets teachers apart, simply because of their age, must lead to an ever widening breach. Teachers and students both resort to this explanation, almost these very words. The 'generation gap' owes its superficial plausibility to the fact that it echoes the popular language in which young people assert their differences. The teacher is 'out of touch', rambles on, repeats himself. Ever faithful to an 'out of date' programme, he gathers over his head all the ridicule which certain, more understanding parents manage to dodge. But the teacher who 'no longer' understands his pupils and who does not understand that they no longer understand him is for most of the time also hiding behind this same explanation. When he was 'their age', he took an interest in true culture; he read, discovered, and worked; whereas his pupils at best display an erudition and a passion only for jazz and film.[11] On this account, the clear gap between the cultural values and models of teachers and those of their students is due simply to a 'cultural lag' in which society outstrips the education system at an ever increasing pace.

Adolescent subculture is in fact very unequally distant from the 'culture' of the cultivated class of adults (and thus teachers). How much distance there is depends on the social class of the family to which the adolescent belongs. Upper-class students display a disposition to erudite knowledge and eclectic taste akin to the kinds of habits which school requires, or at least encourages, and which can bè seen in domains of learning which are quite removed from academic orthodoxy. Working-class and middle-class students, on the other hand, often fail to adapt to the demands of the school system, despite a cultural goodwill which is manifest in a thousand ways. In reality, the gap between the generations owes its form and its sharpness to the breach between the social classes which it conceals. Teachers discover tastes and interests in their pupils which are typical of working-class or middle-class adolescents and which astonish them not as members of the 'older generation', but as members of a cultured class to which they often belong by birth.[12]

But the teacher's self-assured use of professorial language is no more fortuitous than the student's tolerance of semantic fog. Quite apart from the fact that individual words, little known or unknown, always appear in a context which imparts a sense of familiarity to them or at least the feeling that they have already been heard before, the whole corpus of professorial language is employed in an environment dominated by the teaching situation with its distinctive space, its ritual, and its temporal field. And if the isolated and voluntary efforts of teachers to break with the pedagogical fiction sound few echoes of sympathy among students, given that it is from teachers that these initiatives come, this is because the most influential factors underlying and perpetuating linguistic misunderstanding are embedded in the very nature of the institution itself. Everything in the present organization of university teaching – from the physical form and layout of the lecture theatre to the examinations regime and its criteria, from the assignments leading up to the exams to the organization of the *curriculum*[13] – favours the reciprocal distancing of teacher and student.

Space and distancing

Space is a source of pedagogical distance, and it is not simply in the most external aspects of the teaching relationship that this logic of establishing distance is realized. It is in all the particularities in which the academic institution locates the teacher – the rostrum, the chair from which a French professor holds forth, his position at the point where all attention converges – that he finds the material conditions to keep his students at a distance, to require and enforce respect, even when, left to himself, he would decline it. Physically elevated and enclosed within the magistral chair which consecrates him, he is separated from his audience by a few empty rows. These physically mark off the distance which the profane crowd, silent before the *mana* of the word, timorously respects and abandons to the most well-trained zealots, pious lesser priests of the professorial word. *Deus absconditus*, remote and untouchable, protected by obscure and alarming spiritual 'authorities' (so many mythologies to him), the professor is in fact condemned by an objective situation more coercive than the most imperious regulation to dramatic monologue and virtuoso exhibition.[14]

The chair from which a lecture emanates takes over the tone, the diction, the delivery and the oratorical action of whoever occupies it, whatever his personal wishes. Thus the student who delivers a paper in place of his professor inherits the rhetorical manners that go with the chair. So rigorously does the physical situation govern the behaviour of both students and lecturers that attempts to establish dialogue between them quickly degenerate into fiction or farce. Questions to the audience are often mere rhetorical gestures, belonging to the exposition, rather than interrupting it (except for a pause for breath). The lecturer can call on students to get involved or voice objections, but there is really no risk of this ever happening. As one student put it, 'Lecturers have a way of asking, "Is that clear?", which actually rules out any question that it might not be clear.' Destined above all to play the part of the faithful at a church service, students must answer with ritual responses.

Students sometimes call for a subversion of this professorial space in favour of round-table exchanges, open dialogue, or 'non-directive' teaching. However, in many of their most deeply held attitudes they remain firmly wedded to the traditional teaching situation. For this also protects *them*, and it is one of the few models of scholastic behaviour open to them. As few attempts are made to introduce new approaches to teaching, most students remain faithful to the traditional space of communication, even in their imagination. Without categories in which innovations could be conceptually explored, they simply hope for more physical comfort in lectures, better visibility of the lecturer, greater audibility – all technical aspects which serve only to confirm the lecturer's privileged position.[15] The overwhelming majority of students do not think past various versions of how teaching space has been traditionally organized. The round-table arrangement, very rarely nominated, is put forward as a kind of challenge, but is then recanted. The conservatism of some students is quite explicit. They want to maintain a distance which guarantees their independence. Most are content with a suitably pious call for freeing up exchanges between lecturer and student, and do not demand the changes that would make this possible. The most revolutionary attitudes end up in self-defeating utopianism, or shamefully restore the traditional teaching relationship.

But if the imagination cannot break free of the existing academic order, this is not a sign of passive acquiescence. Some students design the ideal lecture theatre in the form of a circle whose centre is the lecturer. Thanks to its very ambiguity, this scheme perhaps reveals one of the truths about the relationship which students have with their teachers. From one perspective, the plan of the circle culminates the utopian search for the greatest proximity to the lecturer of the greatest number of students, with the circle simply completing the semicircular amphitheatre. But there are a number of cases, as this extract from a student questionnaire shows, in which the plan betrays an aggressive irony:

> The lecture theatre to be like a theatre-in-the-round. Advantages: much greater intimacy. The lecturer is closer. Contacts are more direct. He doesn't always face the students, but walks around, inspires them. Another advantage: the student always lives in hope that the lecturer will end up like the scorpion in a circle of burning twigs – it stings itself.[16] If the lecturer doesn't want to play scorpions, console yourself watching him go mad trying to escape the innate cruelty of the audience.

The lecturer at the centre of the circle is also the encircled lecturer, the lecturer surrounded, the lecturer turning in a circle. The theme of the encircled lecturer appears more frequently among the responses of students in Paris. There, thanks to the very large number of students, the teaching relationship is more stretched, and the feeling of abandonment more pronounced. In this context the image captures the truth of a system in which outward passivity does not exclude a masked aggression. If it is true that a student's relationship to his teacher owes its emotional tone to the fact that it always tends to reactivate the paternal relationship, we should not forget that other factors are involved which run just as deep. These build the teaching relationship into the structures of the intellectual personality, especially among intellectuals.[17] For it is through the teacher that socially recognized hierarchies and our place within them are established. To these hierarchies of intelligence and culture, no one, whatever he says, can remain indifferent. The teaching relationship offers students values which are a major source of personal security, and provides a platform not only for their professional futures and social success, but for the esteem in which they are held by others and for their own self-esteem.[18]

That the space of the teaching relationship imposes its law of distance so strongly is because it captures and expresses so much of what the university, as an institution, stands for. The values of the academic tradition achieve outward, material form in the way in which the space of the lecture theatre is constructed. However, these same values reappear in other ways of organizing teaching space, thanks to the inertia of institutionalized relationships, and give rise to a virtual space, which pre-exists and in a way is more real than the actual configurations. Thus, in a university which retains its traditional identity in all other respects, round-table teaching fails to stop expectations and attention converging on one individual. It is he who has guarded all the signs of professorial status, beginning with the privilege of speaking and the implied privilege of controlling the speech of others.

Complicity in misunderstanding

The whole system of education as a particular historical structure finds expression in the communication which takes place between teachers and students. Misunderstanding and the fiction that there is no misunderstanding are inseparable phenomena. For, given the way universities recruit, how they exercise control, and how they organize teaching, communicative breakdown and the myth that this does not occur are inherent in the functioning – the malfunctioning – of the institution itself, and contribute to its perpetuation. Academics and students can walk away from the system, but at their own cost. Stay within the system, and their attitudes and behaviour will continue to express the particular logic of its operations. The lecturer can renounce the professorial monologue only by abdicating a portion of his security. He cannot be sure that this step forward will be supported by the emergence of a rational organization of teaching, while the student can mostly respond only with verbal sympathy. Thus the logic of the teaching situation, which chooses lecturer and student more than they choose it, is such that they *owe it to themselves* to overestimate how much information actually circulates in pedagogical communication. Consequently, the most tried and true methods are employed to mask the misunderstanding that unites them. If professors and students have given up any attempt to transform the teaching relationship into a genuine intellectual exchange, a lingering nostalgia for the Socratic dialogue suggests that this is not for want of hope. Rather, it is because an exchange in which the flow of information can be monitored and controlled presupposes access to the techniques of verbal exchange – to methods of relating to the words of the speech partner as well as to one's own words – and these can be acquired only through apprenticeship.

The magistral lecture from the professorial chair and the student essay are *functionally related*, rather than isolated, acts of communication. So, too, are the solo performance of the assistant lecturer and the solitary prowess of the examination candidate, and the discourse *de omni re scibili* and the verbose generalities of essay rhetoric. Substitute explicit and limited demands for today's programmes which have neither horizons nor shores; replace essays with more rigorous and more focused exercises; abandon tests of cultural manners judged according to the most diffuse criteria; and implement assessment practices with built-in monitoring of teacher judgement – introduce all these functionally related reforms, and the fiction that professorial lectures are understood and are effective would immediately fall to pieces. The academic institution is able to forestall this extremity because while students and their lecturers have a theoretical and long-term interest in challenging how universities work, they also have a practical and short-term stake in preserving a fiction which performs vital functions for them in a situation in which they have to act and of which they are the product. For the teacher to accurately measure student comprehension would involve assessing himself on the basis of rational expectations. But he has not received any methodical and specialized training to meet these demands. For the students, every effort to make learning requirements explicit and to assess work with greater accuracy is likely to be greeted as an aggravation of rigour and severity. Again, the lecturer who foregoes the marvels of professorial language and gives methodical and explicit presentations risks appearing as a primary school teacher who has strayed into higher education or as a non-conformist who will also find the institution turned against him, even though he has answered real needs and unacknowledged expectations.

Similarly, the student who, in preparing an essay under the present assessment regime, gives up all the protections and securities that come from emulating the rhetoric of his lecturers and abandons the techniques of distancing the examiner through false generalities and prudent approximations that are *not even wrong* – in short, the student who risks exposing the exact level of his understanding and knowledge by using the clearest possible code of communication – gives up the chance of *assuring* (as they say) *a mark between 9 and 11.* Unless saved by exceptional talent, he necessarily pays the price of clarity.[19] Students who are least apt at deciphering the language of teaching can always rewrite a version of the lecture for the benefit of the lecturer in which no unmistakable nonsense ever stands out. For the essay-writing genre which the university puts at the disposal of the students authorizes the practice of an *ars combinatoria* of the second degree and at second hand, and this generally involves only the manipulation of a finite bunch of semantic atoms, chains of mechanically linked words.

If essay-writing rhetoric gives the lecturer the overall feeling that he is not *too badly* understood, this is because the essay lends itself by its very logic to a discourse designed to inhibit clear-cut choices and to encourage in the examiner judgements as prudent as the material he is correcting. Here the gap between experience and the objective truth of the experience is perhaps never as great. Every academic has experienced the difficulty of marking the mass of mediocre and middling scripts which offer no purchase for clear judgement and which become the object of the most laborious deliberations just to extract, at the end of the day and in despair of any plausible grounds, a verdict of indulgence tainted with scorn: 'Give him a pass' or 'Let him through'. The essay is so poorly 'discriminating' and so suited to hiding ignorance under the cover of mediocrity. Yet, were teachers to set topics or tasks which were capable of delivering a meaningful mark, they would surely be turning against their most habitual practice. The annals of arts examinations are there to testify that academics are faithful to the tradition of setting topics of the most general kind. For it is these which are reputedly able to measure the most general and the most authentic of qualities, those that distinguish the person.

The traditional instruments of communication between students and teachers – presentations and essays – thus appear to have the latent function of preventing a precise measure of student comprehension and of distinguishing this from the mnemonic repetition (*écholalie*) of professorial words which mask misunderstanding. Most students are unable to define terms which appear with high frequency in the language of lectures and essays. This shows that the illusion of being understood, the illusion of understanding and the illusion of having always understood are mutually reinforcing, and supply alibis to each other. Student comprehension thus comes down to a general feeling of familiarity. Any particular concept is illuminated by the same cluster of words, which in turn depend on the context. Rather than forming a unified idea, the concept appears as a constellation of semantic impressions which are linked through mutual consonance and resonance, and produce an irreducible impression of familiarity. This is precisely because the student listening to a lecture understands a sentence in which a succession of technical terms and references, like 'epistemology', 'methodology', 'Descartes', and 'sciences', shoulder each other up. He can quite naturally refrain from seeking clarification of each one of these terms, taken separately; for his system of needs is not, cannot be, and up to a point *must* not be, analytical.[20] Thanks to the same mechanism, the student is able to put together, in his turn, and with little likelihood of appearing absurd, an essay which is apparently written in the same language of ideas, but in which the sentence 'Descartes renewed epistemology and methodology' can only be an impressionistic restoration. For outside this sentence, many students associate nothing with the word 'epistemology'.[21]

Analysis of essay rhetoric brings to light pathological forms of verbal restitution. The essay-writer reinstates the professorial word through processes of levelling, reinterpretation and decontextualization which point not to a cultural apprenticeship at work, but to the logic of acculturation.[22] The typical essay is characterized by a discourse of allusion and ellipsis. This presupposes student complicity in and through the linguistic misunderstanding which today defines the teaching relationship. Transmitting information in a language which is little understood or is not understood, the lecturer should not, by all logic, be able to understand what his students transmit back to him. But the lecturer who suspects the limits of student comprehension without admitting it and without drawing all the consequences, the lecturer who feels he has the statutory authority to hold his students responsible when he does not understand their comments, is no more truly concerned to understand what they are saying and what they want to say than they themselves know what they are saying and what they wish to say. He expects them to really say something as little as they really hope to have anything to say. Indeed, there is nothing that he requires of the language of students except that it 'point to' a possible discourse, the complete knowledge and comprehension of which lie with him alone. This applies to the thoughts of particular authors, as well as to his own ideas. Students adjust perfectly to this discourse which can be read from hints, because it is necessarily the lecturer, not the student, who is supposed to possess the balance of the words unsaid. 'I don't understand what students write,' one academic admits. 'Or at least I get the feeling I shouldn't understand. Of course I do know what they're getting at because I know the last word in the story – it's the same story that I told them. The sloppy way they use technical terms is worrying, but we fill in the gaps.'

Duality and ambiguity

Given what a system of education sets out to achieve, it is unquestionably pathological that a teacher should expect his words to be understood precisely as he understands them and that the language of his students should merely echo his own. Such an expectation is inherently contradictory and dualistic. In fact, academics display two complementary and contradictory attitudes. They address themselves to fictive subjects, avoiding the risk of putting their teaching practice on trial. It is up to the student to cover the whole of the ground, and if he does not live up to the being which he ought to be – his 'being-for-the-teacher' – the mistakes are always wholly attributable to him, whether out of error or out of spite. Addressing the student as he ought to be, teachers unfailingly discourage him from asserting his right to be only what he is. Moreover, they are able to justify their disdain for the real student, since only the fictive student deserves their respect, and a handful of 'gifted students' – objects of all their care – prove that the fiction exists. Once good pupils themselves, it is to good pupils that they now address themselves; and for their pupils they would have only future teachers.[23] And when the real world of students comes too manifestly to the surface – on those rare occasions when the quality of communication is actually monitored – teachers can always exorcize the spell of misunderstanding by ritualistically deploring it. They thereby evade all the implications that would have to be drawn from the failure of communication were there a willingness to look at the situation rationally. 'They understand nothing,' 'The standard is again lower than last year.' The sorrowful recognition and the sorrowful proclamation of linguistic misunderstanding play the same role and produce the same effects as wilful ignorance. By superimposing on the same period what every teacher remembers having always said and always having heard said, and by reaffirming permanence in change, the tragic deploring of the 'continuing decline in standards' takes on the functions, through its very stereotyping, of a rite of reassurance.

Periodically called to mind, 'bad students' are like evil in theodicies. They keep us from feeling that we are in the best of all possible worlds. But they also justify using the pedagogical manners that would be desirable in the best of all possible worlds. For this objective evil furnishes the sole unimpeachable excuse for the failure of the teaching relationship, by portraying it as inevitable. Professorial diatribes are thus perhaps above all apologetical positions. Revolt against the 'incompetence' of students – theologians speak of 'nothingness' or 'wretchedness' – is a way of making this nullity an eternal and ineluctable necessity, against which no rational or reasonable action can be opposed. Bad pupils are at one and the same time the truth and the justification of the system of education which consigns them to hell.

The objective situation in which students find themselves compels them to enter into the game of fictive communication. To play the game, they must embrace the vision of the academic world which casts them in a state of unworthiness. Just as in the Kula cycle, in which armshells only ever circulate in one direction and necklaces in the other, fine speeches (and fine words) always go from teachers to students, while poor language (and bad jokes) go from students to teachers. If students would not even dream of interrupting a professorial monologue which they do not understand, this is because the part of them that obeys the logic of the situation reminds them that if they do not understand, then they should not be present. From the first year of secondary school, students are required above all not to deny the fiction of linguistic understanding which the academic world needs in order to function. Obligatory resignation in approximate understanding is the precondition of their adaptation to this system, and at the same time its product. Since they are supposed to understand, since they ought to have understood, the idea that they have a right to understand escapes them. So they must be content with lowering the level of what they can expect to understand. 'You think to yourself – I should understand this, everybody else does. But later on you find out when talking among yourselves that no one else understood either. "I'll have to go over this later," you say. You can't follow it at first, but once you've gone over your notes, you'll pick it up.'

To admit incomprehension or only half-comprehension, the student has to retreat from the flattering light of the ideal being which good pupils must strive to be and which the high tone of the professor at least assumes to be present before him. The serial group of co-disciples acts as a censor which obliges each of them to withhold his questions out of fear of appearing naïve or ridiculous. Imitating the good pupil – for everyone can imitate without imitating any one person in particular – the student is hidden in the amorphous audience of the lecture theatre. This is the privileged site for a reciprocal inhibition of communication which relies on mutual mystification and which is completely contrary to learning through emulation, even though it relies on an ethos of competition.[24] '"There's also the fear of being laughed at." By whom? The lecturer or other students? "Other students, in the first place. Some of us aren't particularly brilliant and don't want to look like imbeciles. And then if you interrupt the lecturer you look a complete fool. . . . So a kind of self-censorship operates."'

Fear of not measuring up to a student ideal which each of the co-disciples huddled together in the anonymity of the lecture theatre might have attained obliges each to measure himself against the ideal without ever betraying his distance from it. Through the stereotyped rhetoric of collective blame, the professor avoids clear and open assessments of the teaching situation which would contradict the image of the perfectly comprehending pupil which he presupposes and wants to project. The student, for his part, can only be grateful to his teacher for a discretion which frees him from having to face the truth. These fictions offer the teacher protection from day to day; but he must pay through a deeper insecurity. Obvious signs of success elude him. A siege mentality is the only way he can avoid admitting failure.

Spatial distance and verbal distance

The ambiguous relationships of teachers and students towards linguistic misunderstanding contribute to its perpetuation. So long as their attitudes remain complementary, despite external tensions, this can continue. Distancing gives as much protection to the student as the professor. Entrenched in the magistral chair from which he holds forth, the professor is enclosed by it. If he addresses no one in particular, neither can he blame anyone personally. Without collective sanctions, a responsibility which is diffuse turns into no one's responsibility. The student, too, remains deeply attached to the traditional teaching relationship and to the sites and instruments which distinguish it. His search for 'reconciliation' with a remote professor only rarely involves a wish to reduce the obligatory distance which separates them. The professor, engaged in a monologue on a topic chosen by him, prepared and physically removed from his silent interlocutors, is sheltered from the hazards of improvisation, from surprise interruptions and from objections that might be fired at him. He knows the insecurity inherent in a role which, periodically and at fixed hours, obliges a series of acts of virtuosity. It is understandable that he should seek to mobilize every defence that language can offer him. Indeed, language is the most effective and the most subtle of all the techniques of distancing. By comparison with the distance achieved by manipulating space or that legislated by regulation, the distance which words create seems to owe nothing to the academic institution as such. The magistral chair, physically separate from the person, can offer only rudimentary protection. Language, on the other hand, appears as the action and emanation of the person himself. But the professorial word really owes most of its effects to the institution. For it is a pure product of academic training, and it can never be dissociated from the teaching situation in which it comes to life. Enough, it is, that the word not appear as the attribute of an institution for it to fulfil its primary function, to turn to the profit of the person of the functionary the advantage of the function.

The professor has been able to abandon the ermine and the toga; he can even enjoy descending from his rostrum to mix with the crowd. But he cannot abdicate his ultimate protection, the professorial use of a professorial language.[25] School is a universe of language, and of the professor one can say with Plato, 'He is not man, he is speech.' He is the one who speaks *upon* things, instead of speaking *about* them. Again, there is nothing upon which he cannot hold forth, the class struggle or incest, because his situation, his person and his rank 'neutralize' his remarks.[26] The language which is capable of performing this function is inseparable from a particular type of teaching relationship – traditional or charismatic – or, as is more frequently encountered in the literary disciplines, the traditional-charismatic. In charismatic teaching, or 'education through awakening' – as happens in magical initiations – language is first and foremost a marvellous incantation whose whole justification lies in placing the disciple in a fit state to receive grace. Ceremonial speeches, 'public seminars', lectures at the Collège de France, give a clear illustration of this displacement of the role of language. Speech points to itself, rather than to what it formally signifies. For both orator and auditor, all attention is turned away from the signified. Traditional teaching uses words to seduce. Through a process of osmosis, it promotes the transmission of an already confirmed and legitimate culture, and secures commitment to the values which this contains. Charismatic and traditional teaching stand in marked contrast to the rational use of language, which is suited to democratic education. The language of illusion in charismatic teaching can transmit only an illusion of its true value. In traditional teaching, the language of allusion presupposes a community of language between master and pupil and an already established complicity in values, and this occurs only when education is concerned with its own heirs.

Summoned to defend himself with words in a combat wherein not all words are permitted, what can the student do but turn to the rhetoric of despair, revert to the ritual use of language, to the mechanical reiteration of ideas presumed dear to his professor, to a caricature of learned discourse, only the padding or a few passwords of which survive? Faithful to a logic of prophylactic rites, prudence or false prudence govern his every step into over-relativism (usually mere non-committal compromise), into false examples and false abstractions which are 'not even wrong', into an imprecision in which the possibility of truth or error vanishes. The propitiatory ritual of erudite citation pays homage to celebrated masters or to culture, and intellectual words play the part of 'sesame'. The rhetoric of despair answers the anxiety generated by a teaching relationship in which the possibility of acquiring technical mastery has been denied. To see that students take their studies with dramatic seriousness, we need only consider their dramatic relationship with professorial language as they seek to write in it. Their despairing imitations display the logic of *nativistic movements*.[27] Blind adherence to a system which withholds the intellectual means of adherence ends in a system of reference which is misrecognized.

* * *

In the traditional pedagogical relationship, the measure of output of information is in itself a measure of the effectiveness of teaching. For in the literary disciplines, at least, teaching comes down to an exchange of words. It takes the form of a verbal exhibition which is more like the *epideixis* of the Sophists than the display exercises of the classroom monitor. There is no place in this mode of teaching for mechanical demonstration or for apprenticeship through imitation, repetition and rehearsal. Carried out under today's conditions, the logic peculiar to traditional teaching is driven to the point of pathology. With 100 students – or 50, if the rules are observed – what we call 'practical classes' become 'small' magistral lectures. On the principle that our awareness of the sickness of a system should confirm its underlying health, once the nature of the teaching relationship is challenged, in part because of the material conditions, it is these that are made the scapegoat.

Professor and student can continue to exchange only lectures and essays, in a circulation of words which sees an ever increasing loss of information, and the professor can lecture as if teaching ends in speech making, because the logic of the academic institution authorizes them to do so. Of all the professorial duties, transmission by speech is the only one which is felt to be an unconditional imperative. It takes precedence over assessing the work of students. The correction of examination papers is often viewed as the dark side of teaching, and is left to assistants. Organizing the work of students is avoided even more. Even the terms that we use to distinguish the ranks of university teachers show that speaking gathers more and more legitimacy as we ascend the hierarchy of appointments. The *assistant* will continue to take 'practical classes', even though all he does is speak; the *chargé d'enseignement* gives a course of instruction; but the *maître de conférences*, who does just the same, nevertheless gives 'lectures'; while the full professor alone gives 'magistral lectures' [*cours magistraux*, lectures *ex cathedra* – trans.].[28] It is obvious how this stratification of teaching ranks also establishes the scale of intellectual tasks. The accomplished intellectual feat, freed of subordinate duties, contrasts with the laborious techniques of intellectual labour. Such a hierarchy can only encourage students to scorn rational techniques of study; for the one institution which can teach these in a rational and meaningful way actually relegates them to the bottom of the hierarchy.

What the student produces from the instructional process is also purely verbal: he, too, pays with words, because only words pay. Obvious in the literary disciplines but more subtle in the sciences, the ability to manipulate academic language remains the principal factor in success at examinations. Here we encounter one of the most important, though also the most hidden, mediations between the social origins of children are their scholastic fates. The linguistic setting of the family influences a broader range of behaviours than those captured by language tests. Performance on every test of intellectual skills which requires the decipherment or manipulation of complex linguistic structures depends on an apprenticeship in language which is unequally complex, according to family background.[29] Moreover, what we inherit from our social origins is not only a language, but – inseparably – a relationship to language and specifically to the value of language. Everything tends to suggest that the further we ascend the social hierarchy, the greater the tendency to verbalize feelings, opinions and thoughts. The attitude to language cultivated in upper-class homes bears a close affinity to an education which demands a generalized 'verbalization' of experience. It did not escape Sartre that a childhood spent in a world in which words tended to become the reality of things prepared him to enter an intellectual world founded on the same principle.

Rationalizing the uses of language in teaching could constitute a decisive step forward in democratizing the academic universe. We have shown elsewhere that every effort to limit and to define the underlying requirements of student learning and student reporting of their learning by making assessment practice rational and explicit reduces the disadvantages suffered by the most disfavoured groups without favouring any one group in particular. Every effort in the direction of an agreement on the criteria of success to be used in examinations and on the nature of the assessment tasks themselves would doubly minimize the handicaps experienced by the disinherited – first, by reducing the importance of diffuse intellectual manner and scholastic know-how, and second, by assigning to each assessment task an explicit aim and justification and a clear framework of expectations. Now all these changes presuppose that the university teacher adopt an absolutely novel attitude towards both his own use of language and that of his students. The teacher cannot step out of his linguistic and cultural 'ethnocentrism' to discover that the language he spontaneously employs is that of a particular social class without seeing at the same time that the language his students spontaneously employ also owes its essential characteristics, whether approved or reproved, to their social origins. It goes without saying that this realization must not, and cannot, lead to the abdication of all linguistic demands. On the contrary, it should lead to providing students with the means of satisfying these demands. What matters is to make the presuppositions underlying the academic manipulation of language as explicit as possible, so as to make the explicit transmission of these demands possible. Professorial language, for example, would change in meaning and function – even without changing vocabulary or syntax – were there a concern at every moment with definition and with verifying the real comprehension needs of a real public.[30]

Such a *conversion* in attitude to the language of teaching clearly also implies a complete conversion in attitude to those being taught. Instead of addressing his remarks to the ideal student, the teacher would need to plan his language according to an informed view of what students are really like. There is a world of difference between the traditional approach to definition which is purely formal and ritualistic – and is reproduced and caricatured in student essays – and an interactive approach which accepts the ongoing possibility of interruption, interrogation and demand for clarification. To achieve such a conversion in attitudes is likely to be all the more difficult because the teaching relationship as it operates today offers no support. A spontaneous commitment is needed to *act as if* there is a real call on the teacher to share with his students at each moment both the message and the code of the message. But in any event, if the teacher sticks to the linguistic requirements that at present govern his discourse, rather than submitting his language to the demands of explicitness, he prevents students as they really are from meeting his requirements and continues to saddle himself with contradictory expectations.

The whole of our previous analysis suggests that the propositions aimed at a rational teaching practice which flow from it remain strictly utopian under present conditions. It would be contradictory to suggest that they could be implemented except through the spontaneous conversion of academics (and students) acting within the logic of the system of which they are the products. Everything in the conduct, the attitudes and the opinions of academics (and students), becomes clear when referred to the logic of the system, even criticism of the system itself.[31] It is the logic of the system which dominates the ways in which the actors represent the system and its failings, and which also establishes the limits of this representation. Thus, even in their most utopian images, students and academics remain imprisoned by the logic of the institution in its present form. If their fictive images of another possible system are so impoverished, it is because the objective deficiencies of a system cannot appear in their true guise to the human subjects who are trapped in it and subject to it. Because the academic system is never seen as the system of interdependence that it really is, the diagnoses put forward by its partners remain caught in dichotomies that permit them to pass praise and blame back and forth to one another indefinitely.

These mechanisms rest on a fundamental complementarity of behaviour which inevitably assumes the outward appearance of *complicity* between teachers and taught. Their complicity is all the more scandalous in that, behind the projects of teaching and learning in which they are outwardly engaged, it is the objective truth. An objective product fashioned by the actors themselves, in which they prefer not to see what they set out to make, seems foreign to their intentions only till we remember that the twisted relationship of each of the partners with himself in fact assured it. By refusing any real measure of the quality of communication between them, teachers and students enter into an agreement, and this does not presuppose some kind of contract, even an unconscious one. Each individual stands in a relationship of bad faith towards the role he plays. He knows there is misunderstanding, and also that he must carry on as if there were not. For otherwise he would be compelled to abandon the benefits of maintaining it. Thus teacher and student find in the relationship of their partner to the environment of misunderstanding the best way of perpetuating the relationship that each has with himself.

What makes this objective complicity possible, as the intersection of the complicity of each partner with himself, is the fact that the ideological relationship of student and teacher to their own practices operates with reference to the same objective end. They are the products of a traditional system, which focuses on maximizing security. But at the same time they are located in a society and at a level in this society where the values of rationality are imposed as key points of reference. Professor and student, even when their demands on the teaching relationship clash, can therefore only acquiesce in a system of deep expectations in which the desire to maximize *output* refuses to pay the price of abandoning *security*. The professor, to take just one example, can retain the comfort and the gratifications of prestige which come from delivering lectures *ex cathedra*, and at the same time exhort his students to be more active; while, for their part, students can retain, as his complicit adversaries, the security of anonymity and the satisfactions of dilettantism, all the while vehemently demanding a total revolution in teaching. Just like those farmers in cultural transition who would like to accumulate the advantages of the two economic systems they stand between – the high yield of the tractor and the low risks of the plough – academics and students are placed in a system under threat, and are held in thrall by the system which threatens them. The locus of conflicting tendencies, they want the protections of the rostrum, but at the same time the fruitful exchanges of the round table.

APPENDIX: SELECTED RESULTS FROM THE IDEAL LECTURE-THEATRE TEST

The teaching relationship and projected methods of teaching[32]

Teaching methods can be grouped into four broad categories,[33] depending on the mode of transmission and the degree of technical intervention [see table 1]:

1   *First-generation methods*, which involve a transfer of information without the intervention of machines (either for reproduction or for transmission). These methods include:
    (a)   oral demonstrations and presentations by the teacher;
    (b)   instruments connected with this mode of transmission; blackboard, graphics, drawings, displays.

2   *Second-generation methods*, which mobilize the possibilities of printing as a reproduction technology:
    (a)   books (manuals, texts, tests);
    (b)   the apparatus of resources connected with these (libraries, archives).

3 *Third-generation methods*, or 'audio-visual', in which machines are substituted for the teacher. Audio-visual methods perform the functions of *visualization* (photography, screen, projections), *listening* (radio), or *seeing and listening* at the same time (film, television). Equipment includes screens, fixed and portable projectors, television sets, tape recorders.

4 *Fourth-generation methods*, which establish a direct relationship between individuals and machines; e.g., 'self-instructional programmes' and 'language laboratories'.

Bearing in mind that, in France, higher education institutions almost exclusively employ first-generation methods, the teaching ideal entertained by students would appear to be more an expression of current conditions than of hopes or expectations about future possibilities.

Despite an express invitation to think in utopian terms and to exclude any 'cost' considerations, university students remained attached even in their imaginations to the traditional type of communication. The instrument most often mentioned in their responses is none other than the blackboard. If any appeal at all is made to the possibilities opened up by modern communications technologies, this is mostly to improve the audibility of the professorial lecture (using a microphone or loudspeaker), rather than to augment communication by additional methods of information, documentation or illustration (films, overhead projector, recordings).

Finally, second-generation methods are mentioned least often. The idea of the specialized library which converts the 'lecture theatre' into a 'theatre of work' only rarely appears. Doubtless this is because, once again, an ideal of teaching is projected only from within the system of actual practices, which operates as an inescapable framework.

Pedagogical rigidity in university students is all the more remarkable because at least in one sense the invitation to present a teaching utopia was clearly understood. The most up-to-date or revolutionary techniques are frequently introduced, but *exclusively* to improve comfort and passive well-being. These are 'science fiction' responses in which the customary way of being in a class is completely overturned (transparent partitions, gardens, gallery tours, *avant-garde* architecture). But the class of the year 2000 still sees the traditional lecture unrolling before it. When it comes to comfort, in other words, students think in terms of the twenty-first century; but when they think of teaching, it is in terms of the nineteenth century [see table 2].

Although we should not be too surprised by the fact that all the responses are developed from the image of the lecture (for the instruction contained the expression 'lecture theatre'), it is remarkable that the answers which seem the most innovative introduce only extra-pedagogical aspects (comfort and various touches associated with this). Aspirations are limited to making changes in the conditions of reception of the professorial lecture [see table 3], a theme which appears almost obsessive in the longest responses, and which at any rate is always more frequent among girls than boys.

Table 1 Teaching methods favoured by university students

Type of teaching methods selected by students[a]		Males (%) (n = 85)	Females (%) (n = 86)	Persons (%) (n = 171)
First-generation	Lectures	100	100	100
	Blackboard	49.4	53.5	51.4
	Microphone & loud-speaker	27.0	25.6	26.3
Second-generation	Library Books Archives }	5.9	17.4	11.7
Third-generation	Television or projectors or tape-recorders or record-players	17.6	16.3	17.0
Fourth-generation	Reference to 4th-generation methods	nil	nil	nil

[a] Information from pictorial and written responses combined.

Table 2 Bold approaches to technical design

Responses introducing recent or anticipated technical possibilities	Males (%)	Females (%)	Persons (%)
To improve audibility in lecture theatre and visibility of the lecturer	32.9	27.9	30.4
To improve comfort (seating, air-conditioning, etc.)	34.1	36.0	35.1
To revolutionize architecture of lecture theatre	18.8	14.0	16.4
To introduce various whims (pedagogically gratuitous)	14.1	7.0	10.5
To transform teaching relationship	3.5	2.3	2.9

The circle plan

This configuration, an idealized extension of the semicircular lecture theatre, perfectly expresses the utopian logic according to which the optimum is confounded with the maximum in all domains. If the circle plan formally answers the imper-

Table 3 Reception conditions for the lecture

Aim of responses	Males (%)	Females (%)	Persons (%)
Hearing the lecturer clearly	37.6	41.8	39.8
Being able to see the lecturer	40.0	59.3	52.0
Being able to write comfortably	32.9	34.9	33.9

ative of increasing the proximity between teacher and students, it also carries to the point of paroxysm the traditional attitude which places the teacher at the point of convergence of attention, and thus makes teaching a spectacle. But, as can be seen from a number of comments, this rational elaboration relies too obviously on the fiction it would rather not be confused with, and through a process of ironical self-distancing, it goes on to release the latent aggression characteristic of the traditional system.

The following are comments by the students:

Everything is based on the fact that the professor has to be at the centre of his pupils. He has to mix with them to get to understand them better. So I believe that a friendship between professor and pupils would develop. That's why I would give this classroom a circular form. What's more, each pupil should feel at ease and be seated so as to be able to see the professor clearly. So I visualize a kind of circular amphitheatre. Such an arrangement would be quite interesting where teaching was oral only. But there would be serious problems where a board was required – unless material was projected onto the roof, like in a planetarium. (Lens – male student, aged 20, final-year *lycée* class)

The lecture theatre to be like a theatre-in-the-round. Advantages: much greater intimacy. The lecturer is closer. Contacts are more direct. Moreover, he doesn't always face the students, but walks about, inspires them. Another advantage: the student always lives in hope that the lecturer will end up like the scorpion in a circle of burning twigs – it stings itself. If the lecturer doesn't want to play scorpions, console yourself watching him go mad trying hopelessly to escape the innate cruelty of the audience. (Lille – male student, aged 20, philosophy student)

Ideal type of ancient arena or cell: nucleus and protoplasm: the tribune is placed at the centre. The orator is visible to everyone and from all sides. Circular tiers advance outward from him, descending high to low; this permits the greatest number of auditors to find a place. The style calls to mind some circular markets (fish) in the south of France: large bay windows to be added (sun, importance of light); a walking path round the top (between lectures); amplifiers; light colours (preferably just one); simple equipment, not too much comfort. (Lille – male student, aged 23, sociology student)

The teacher's desk at the centre of the room, surrounded by tables for the pupils: 1. The teacher can see all his pupils; all his pupils see him and hear him quite distinctly. 2. Circular rooms with light from all sides. 3. The last rows clearly elevated above the first. 4. Rule requiring the teacher not to present his back to anyone. (Lille – female student, aged 21, sociology student)

Area: 6 m × 6 m, height 5 m, 180 m³. This hall is designed for an era of transition between the present situation (teacher-students) and the future (students-teacher). It is thus appropriate to give the teacher a feeling of his powerlessness before the rising generation: put him completely alone in the middle, with his chair, a little elevated, and ten students around him. Numerous doors to allow students who are going off to sleep to slip out. (Paris – male student, aged 18, sociology student)

The tables are set in a ring, so that there is neither extreme left nor extreme right, and consequently no politics. At the centre, the chair or sentry box or bunker of the teacher. The great drawback is that half of the students see only his back; this can be remedied by skilful use of a mirror. In a corner, place the statue of a great scholar or philosopher, so that the teacher will not have the impression of being surrounded wholly by a bunch of cretins. (Paris – male student, aged 20, philosophy student)

1. Teacher's chair rotatable, so that his back is never given to one part of the audience. 2. Roof screened for projection; convertible, allowing students the maximum of fresh air and sun. Projector trained on the teacher when the roof is closed (bad weather). (Paris – male student, aged 22, sociology student)

The students' desks are raised from the centre in concentric circles. A table lamp lights their notebooks. Only the teacher is completely in the light. There must be freedom for students to leave, so that they do not feel like prisoners. The centre should attract them, not block them. The greatest error would be to make available only one exit near the teacher's desk. Not a military parade, but a Socratic spectacle. The teacher's desk should periodically turn to make any fixed image of the teacher impossible. (Paris – male student, aged 21, sociology student)

A room in the form of a circle, the teacher at the centre, talking into a microphone, so as to give a more complete impression of a spectacle. (Paris – male student, aged 21, sociology student)

A sliding partition divides the round amphitheatre into semi-circles; this partition permits better use to be made of the lecture theatre. Nevertheless, the difficulty with such a room is that it is difficult to place a board or a screen in a way that would be visible from the two semi-amphitheatres when these are combined . . . (Paris – male student, aged 21, philosophy student)

The teacher in the middle of the pupils . . . People enter at random. Tape-recorders, to be able to listen to the lecture afterwards, or outside where it was being given . . . (Paris – female student, aged 19, philosophy student)

Students in a circle, teacher in the middle. Permission to smoke. Armchairs as in the theatre, ashtrays at the back of each armchair. Seats in tiers. (Paris – female student, aged 22, philosophy student)

Teacher at the centre, his chair turning at will (to change view) . . . Public address system, individual service, with the possibility of music if teacher irritating. (Paris – female student, aged 21, sociology student)

NOTES

1   It might be different if the act of teaching was traditional in its goals and only used traditional methods. The ambiguity which, in this respect, underlies our education system springs from the fact that, while remaining traditional, it operates in a cultural context dominated by rationalization and the values of rationality.

2   See below, chapter 1.

3   See below, chapter 2.

4   In this respect it may be necessary to qualify what was said above concerning the teaching of philosophy as a privileged domain of explicitness and definition. There exists, in fact, an implicit philosophy of philosophy teachers, expressed above all in a particular relationship to philosophical language: 'Philosophical language is a whole: to define it is to fragment it.' 'The dictionary of Lalande is not a solution.' 'The vocabulary of philosophy will be learnt as a child learns language, by slow osmosis.' This ideology rests on a confusion between the relationships which unite concrete vocabulary to abstract vocabulary (relationships of a kind that allow us to pass from the former to the latter by an apprenticeship which presupposes neither explanation nor exercise) and the relationships uniting the diffuse vocabulary of everyday life with the specific vocabulary of the scientific languages which cannot be acquired by simple 'registration' of the words in their context and which is defined, precisely, by the artificial intention of reacting against this diffuse symbolization.

5   The effort to make the code of the transmission explicit in the course of the transmission itself – i.e., the effort at continued definition, something which is totally repugnant to masters of virtuosity – really comes closest to the pedagogical intention when the teacher is unable to communicate in a code known to the taught, a language easy and already known; but this is possible only in courses for beginners.

6   Reflection on the teaching practice which engenders misunderstanding is quite rare: 'They don't understand us and it is our fault' is something never heard. The interest which academics generally show in the meagre results of

students on vocabulary tests is not without ambiguity. Most seem to react to the student's lack of understanding with a perverse sort of joy, as if linguistic misunderstanding becoming an objectively known fact justified an opinion that they had held all along.

7   [In 1948 a preparatory year in university was introduced, known as the *année propédeutique* (propaedeutical year); its purpose was partly orientation and preparation, and partly to sift out students deemed unsuitable for university studies. Students taking this year were called *propédeutes*, which has been translated as 'preliminary-year students'. The *propédeutique* was abolished in 1966 – trans.]

8   Student expectations can take on an air of positivism, especially in the 'positive' disciplines like the human sciences, without losing any of the nostalgia for total knowledge. Thus we often hear students in the human sciences demanding that a class should go right to indisputable results or to unquestionable techniques, rather than lingering over the examination of methods or discussion of theories. This kind of expectation, which belongs to one esoteric order, clashes with those usually supplied by higher education.

9   A first methodical observation of behaviour at an oral examination leads us to distinguish the verbal ease most directly recognized and most appreciated by the teacher – the one that combines facility of expression with offhandedness of delivery and smoothness of tone – from the forced ease peculiar to working-class and middle-class students who do their best – by volubility of delivery and by not a few discordant tones – to conform to the norms of academic verbalization. This false ease, shot through with an anxiety which stands out all too clearly and dominates, makes its function as a foil too transparent not to be suspected of self-seeking vulgarity in the eyes of teachers wedded to the prestigious fiction of an exchange which, even during examinations, should remain an end in itself.

10 Still, it must be observed that the intemperate use of the language of ideas and the approximating manipulation of professorial language risk reinforcing the illusion of understanding a language whose most difficult and grandiose terms – like 'dialectic', 'model', 'structure', 'transcendental', 'ideology' – are retained in preference to others.

11 Similarly, some sociologists view the modern means of communication (the press, radio, cinema, television) as the principal vehicle for transmitting cultural goods, with traditional education no longer transmitting anything but a vestigial culture, cut off by the living culture. Our survey of the cultural practices and tastes of students has shown that erudition in jazz and cinema is very rare among students, and is most often found among those who are best adapted to the academic world. (Cf. P. Bourdieu and J.-C. Passeron, *Les Étudiants et leurs études*, Cahiers du Centre de sociologie Européenne, no. 1 (Mouton, Paris and The Hague, 1964), pp. 109–19.)

12 The most precise observations of teachers ('They no longer know how to write French' – i.e., academic French) do not necessarily predispose them to undertake an analysis of real changes. In looking back to an indeterminate and mythical past, the alleged conditions of an ideal pedagogy (the 'no . . . longer')

serve to dispense them from any need of a more searching curiosity. The sensitivity of teachers to misunderstanding becomes all the more acute as the social basis of the level of education to which they belong has expanded over one generation. That is to say, it is encountered in secondary education more than in primary education (where teachers, themselves of lower-status origins, have for a long time been accustomed to teaching students from all backgrounds), and more often, too, in higher education.

13 [In Latin in the original, thus a running, a course, a race – trans.]

14 Doesn't the elevated, closed, padded chair of traditional lecture theatres function at least as much to 'conceal' the professor as to dignify him? In fact, only a bust appears, as if everything was done to concentrate attention on the face or, better, on the mouth, the organ of the word.

15 In the appendix a selection of results is presented which illustrate, in particular, the pedagogical conformism concealed beneath a show of futurism. The test, modelled on the *test du village*, was suggested to us by Marcel Maget. It is summed up in the instruction 'Design the ideal lecture theatre and elaborate'.

16 Regarding this image, need we recall what schoolchildren sing: 'Long live holidays, down with punishments, exercise books to the flames and the master in the middle'?

17 Freud writes:

> We now understand our relationship with our teachers. These men, who were not even fathers themselves, became father-substitutes for us. It is for that reason that they appeared so mature, so inaccessible to us, even when they were still very young. We transferred the respect and expectations associated with the omniscient father of our childhood to them and then began to treat them like our fathers at home. Over against them we set the ambivalence we had developed in the family, and with this attitude ranged ourselves against them, just as we were accustomed to struggle against our natural fathers. Without taking into account the context of nursery and family life, we will not understand our behaviour towards the teacher, nor find cause to pardon it. (*Zur Psychologie des Gymnasiasten* (1914), in *Gesammelte Werke*, vol. 10, p. 204 [trans. from the original])

This mechanism of identification perhaps explains the sermonizing so characteristic of examination scripts. Forced to make do, the student selects from his arsenal of commonplaces those that best fit the expectations he has borrowed from his teacher (in other words, the sensible reasonings of Papa holding forth at the dinner table) or those he could use in his capacity as guardian of the wisdom of nations.

18 The wealth and ambiguity of rationalizations to which the teaching relationship gives rise are enough to show that it is highly charged with emotional resonance. There is no social actor (student, teacher, journalist, administrator, parent) who is in a position to deliver an emotionally neutral judgement about and, *a fortiori*, a diagnosis of himself, because there is no individual, at

least in our societies, who has not come within the orbit of school and whose relationships with school, with its hierarchies and its decrees (qualifications not being the only evidence), have not been defined in a multiplicity of ways.

19 The maxims of this morality of prudence are communicated, in a quasi-explicit fashion, in the preparatory classes of the *grandes écoles*, so that, ultimately, the 'higher' rhetoric and the rhetoric of despair turn out to involve the same values. We know, e.g., that the naïvety of naïveties consists in 'writing nothing on the pretext of knowing nothing', and that 'You don't need to know much to get a pass in history', so long as you make sparing use of chronology. Clearly this artful prudence also runs its own risks, as the experience of that student in a preparatory class testifies, who, having read in a chronology *Krach boursier à Vienne* [stock-market crash (*Krach*) in Vienna – trans.] held forth on the *boursier Krach* [stockbroker named Krach – trans.]. When teachers amuse themselves with these pearls, they forget that such misfirings of the system also contain the truth of the system within them. The 'university elite' has been formed in this school, and when we think about this and about all the ethical implications of these exercises, we will come to understand one whole side of *homo academicus* and his intellectual productions.

20 After the administration of a test which included definitions, students were asked why they did not object to terms in lectures which nearly all of them were unable to define. They invariably replied that they 'understood them in context': 'It's a phenomenon of habit. We've always already heard these philosophical terms or very nearly all of them; that's why we always think we recognize them.' But this 'context', as we have seen, is not only the semantic context; it presupposes the whole teaching situation, its constraints and its ritual.

21 Often used in the human sciences and in philosophy, the term 'epistemology' is perhaps sometimes bandied about. But whether it is used correctly or not, in taking it for granted that the term is understood, teachers can protect themselves all the more from their own bad faith by denouncing the word when it reappears in student essays. We can also see how, among students, 'affecting to be understood' leads not only to 'affecting to have understood', but to the subjective certitude of actually having understood, out of respect, as it were, for the teacher and the teaching situation. When the teacher says 'epistemological', or when he reads this word in the work of a student, would he ever dream that among the students whom he believes he is communicating with, some 45% dare not assign any meaning to the word, or only something aberrant, and that only 11% are capable of defining it adequately? Here are a few teratological examples: 'epi-, external, at the surface. Epiphenomenon'. 'It is the study of the relations between different words in the phrase: predicate and attribute.' 'Term in philosophy. Epistemological problem, that is, one which excites written claims and counter-claims.' 'The body of laws permitting us to verify whether hypotheses as put forward are borne out experimentally as originally envisaged.'

22 It is not so much the fact of verbal restitution which needs to be questioned as a means of monitoring communications from teacher to student, but the

specific distortion of the content of communication which occurs through linguistic misunderstanding. As we shall see, the fashionable image of education as ingestion and regurgitation illustrates the logic of the 'not even false'.

23 In fact, when they prepare their lectures with implicit reference to the audience of students from which they themselves were drawn – most of them having been pupils of the *grandes écoles* – they are aiming at the 'elite' (at least on the criteria used in higher education). Pedagogically this situation is paradoxical. For it is the teachers in universities who are most oriented towards research but who lecture to the least-selected students; whereas in the *grandes écoles*, students with the highest aspiration levels and the greatest success meet teachers who are most obedient to pedagogical goals and models derived from school. If the pedagogical intention and, more precisely, the concern to transmit explicitly the techniques of intellectual work are so rare, this is because teachers are often aware of having always known what students do not know: unable to trace back to any of their own teachers in particular the tricks by which they themselves learnt, they forget that they often picked them up in 'peer groups'.

24 Only a very weak intersubjective knowledge could make each co-disciple appear to threaten the other with ridicule or scorn, regardless of what that person's academic results might happen to be, unknown or only badly known. And in fact it would appear that dialogue tends to be established much more easily between students and teachers once students themselves constitute a more integrated group. As soon as an academic hierarchy is established, as in the preparatory classes for the *grandes écoles*, e.g., where not a week goes past without the posting of some results, everyone knows perfectly well who is ahead, and anxiety takes on a different complexion.

25 It is no accident that teachers often stand out first by their tone and second by their language. This is never so apparent as in public situations, where teachers often seem to bring with them their habitual audience of pupils.

26 Many attitudes reveal a perception of the teacher as 'above the ordinary'. For example, if he uses a slang word, this provokes stupor or laughter. Pupils in *lycées* become hysterical at the thought of their teacher swimming or cycling. The image of the teacher which they create in their minds is encapsulated in a formula used by pupils in a provincial *lycée* to characterize their literature teacher in their journal: 'Be as serious as you can, without bursting into laughter, in explaining the comedies that he alone finds funny.'

27 [In English in the original – trans.]

28 We could extend this by saying that in the primary school the teacher 'takes' (prosaically) 'the class' – i.e., practices his craft – while in the *lycée* the teacher (*le professeur*) 'gives lessons' (*fait des cours*). These are that and no more [he does not present 'lectures', *professer des cours* – trans.], because they are not presumed to be professorial.

29 The works of Bernstein show that the linguistic influence of family background is exerted from earliest childhood. Cf. B. Bernstein, 'Some sociological determinants of perception', *British Journal of Sociology*, 9 (1958), pp. 159–74; 'Language and social class', *British Journal of Sociology*, 11 (1960), pp. 271–6; 'Social class and linguistic development', in A. H. Halsey, J. Floud and

C. A. Anderson [eds], *Education, Economy and Society* (Free Press, Glencoe, [Ill.], 1961), pp. 288–314; 'Linguistic codes, hesitation phenomena and intelligence', *Language and Speech*, 5 (1962), pp. 31–46; 'Social class, speech systems and psychotherapy', *British Journal of Sociology*, 15 (1964), p. 54.

30 What is in question here is less a language as such than a relationship to language. Whether it concerns the technical language of an academic discipline, the language of an author or even the language of everyday life, the same language can be handled either in a technical and rational way, as an instrument of communication consciously utilized as such, or in a magical and prophetic way. The language of Husserl is in itself neither more nor less pedagogical than that of Alain, and both could be used to dazzle, to charm or to speak with a view to saying nothing.

31 When the teacher does his best to make the examination process rational, by making learning requirements specific, by making the criteria of assessment explicit, and by organizing tests so that they lead to more precise judgements, he runs into incomprehension at first and then into resistance, due to the fact that innovation, interpreted within the logic of the system, appears as a trap. However, the very anxiety that the examination produces under the present system can induce students to weigh up the advantages which such a contract would give them, to distinguish the explicit formulation of demands from an accumulation of them, and to recognize that rationalization provides a guarantee against unknown risks. Because the perfect functioning of the mechanisms of reciprocal mystification which we have described assumes that students are of bourgeois origin, Parisian residence and have a traditional scholastic background, the consciousness of, or at least the feeling of, malaise is the more readily encountered the further removed students are from this situation. On this basis, acceptance of rational innovation should be more speedy and more complete among working-class and middle-class students, and teaching experiences should be more easily freed from the grip of the system in the provinces than in Paris.

32 The instruction to students was 'Design the ideal lecture room and elaborate'.

33 Cf. W. Schramm, UNESCO Colloquium, 1962.

1

Students and the Language of Teaching

Pierre Bourdieu
Jean-Claude Passeron
Monique de Saint Martin

Do university students understand the language of their teachers? How much does student comprehension depend on social background? To answer these questions, a survey of French university students was carried out during the 1962–3 academic year.[1] Linguistic misunderstanding in the ways that academics and students communicate had already been highlighted in a pilot study.[2] But to confirm this finding required a broader, more systematic approach.

Here we should bear in mind that research aimed at elucidating relationships between test criteria and background factors, rather than describing the distribution of particular behaviour or opinions, can be validly based on a sample whose subgroups are not proportional to their size in the population. Our sample, however, differs very little from arts faculty students generally on key background criteria, such as age, sex and social origins. The dimension of field of study is captured by the two major subgroups in the sample – sociology students and philosophy students – who differ as much as their peers in art history and classics, for example, or psychology and history. However, it is not field of study as such which appears to be the most important stratifying factor, but location of an academic discipline within the institutional hierarchy of studies. The composition of our sample thus permitted us to measure the most relevant attitudinal variations on this underlying dimension as well.[3]

Our concern was to understand and to explain the nature of communication between university teachers and their students – a social phenomenon marked by specific institutional constraints and traditions. Consequently, we could not narrow our goal simply to finding the best mix of predictor variables for various test criteria around which students were normally distributed, without completely abstracting from the institutional and social character of the phenomenon. Academics as a group employ a certain form of language which operates as a given. As a result, they endow a particular set of linguistic requirements with all the objectivity of an institutional fact. It is these demands, then, which should be the criteria in terms of which students are tested if the goal is to determine the extent to which, objectively, they understand what they are objectively supposed to understand.

Our approach was thus to put students systematically into a real assessment situation, as close as possible to examination conditions, rather than to set up an experimental (in fact, fictitious) situation, as standardized tests require. To recreate academic test conditions as far as possible does not imply that examinations are the best measures of ability. But only a test administered under these conditions promises insights into the social factors underlying academic success which teachers measure precisely under these conditions. Far from wishing to legitimate the implicit or explicit criteria used in examinations, we aimed to construct a method for judging teacher assessment itself, and for verifying whether or not the criteria of teacher judgement were socially neutral or, more simply, socially equitable. We deliberately chose, in other words, to lose on formal precision rather than sacrifice our efforts to the abstract principles underlying ability testing, conformity to which would have condemned us, along with most authors of tests, to tautologically defining measured abilities as the things that tests measure.[4]

The academic manipulation of language presupposes a constellation of acquired abilities. To identify the student background factors most commonly associated with ease in the use of language, we divided our language test into a series of exercises which enabled these abilities to be measured separately. With regard to the language of ideas, for example, if a significant proportion of philosophy and social science students in the pilot survey had been unable to define the most frequently occurring terms in this vocabulary,[5] it was likely that they would also have struggled with them in the lectures in which they were actually used. On the other hand, as the language of teaching is remote from other domains of language, depending on the academic discipline, it was desirable to extend our tests to include these other domains as well. For this would establish whether a socially privileged background was linked with greater success in all domains of language or in certain ones only.

Different tests were constructed either from the language of instruction actually used in university lectures or from tests which had already been developed, as in the case of technical language. The aim was to explore two basic dimensions of language use. First, *several domains of vocabulary* were investigated. These ranged from the most academic (tests 1, 2 and 3) to concrete and technical language (test 4), and finally to general culture (test 5). Secondly, several levels of *linguistic behaviour* were examined. These included the comprehension of words in a context (test 1),[6] and extended to the most active forms of verbal manipulation, such as the explicit recognition of words with multiple meanings (polysemia) (test 3), the ability to give a complete formulation of a definition (test 2), and the semi-passive ability to identify the correct definition or the exact synonym from a list. These different forms of relationship to the one language are not all equally indispensable for academic practice (at least in the French context). So the question was whether the ability to perform the most academic tasks was linked with any particular social characteristic, and whether this specific ability also tended to be accompanied by a broader knowledge of concrete vocabulary.

Our survey reveals two fundamental facts: the importance of linguistic misunderstanding in higher education and the determining role of linguistic inheritance in academic success. When tested against learning criteria derived from university teaching practice itself, students show that they have a very imperfect understanding of academic language and even of everyday language.[7] Now it might be objected that, despite some skewness, the test results tend to be normally distributed about a score representing half of all possible errors or around the highest possible mark (depending on the relevant scale), and consequently that the tests yield a pattern of results which differs little from what any test measuring any ability whatever might produce. However, in the tests which measured comprehension or the ability to manipulate academic language, students were confronted with words which in fact were used with high frequency in lectures.[8] Using a word frequently or, even better, without stopping to define it or comment on it is the most objective measure of the lecturer's view that its meaning is understood, or at any rate ought to be understood. Why the evidence of poor comprehension and manipulation skills is so important is because in their instructional practice teachers implicitly expect and impose a requirement of perfect understanding. The gap between teacher expectations and actual student ability is only too obvious from the finding that some of the most common words in the language of ideas are among the most poorly understood. The term 'acceptance' (*acceptation*) is confused with 'meaning' (*acception*) 62 per cent of the time. 'Disinterestedness' (*désintéressement*) is taken for 'lack of interest' (*manque d'intérêt*) by 88 per cent of students. And need we mention the not negligible group who manage to attach to words commonly used in lectures the strangest semantic content? For example, for 'epistemology', 'Studies pertaining to memories, journals (personal), letters. I think epistemology also has something to do with graphology' (female student, aged 20, with three years at university). Or again, 'Study of the origins of linguistic terms' (male student, with six years at university, who took Latin and Greek at school).

But to define the relationship which students have to the professorial language that they understand so badly and that they try to reproduce after a fashion in their essays, we need to go beyond the peculiarly professorial image of students as a socially homogeneous group who differ only according to individual talent and merit. In fact, depending on the language test, most of the social and other background characteristics of students are linked to variations in results [see table 1.1].[9]

Success in literary studies is very closely linked with the ability to manipulate scholastic language, which is a mother tongue only for children

Table 1.1   Scores on five language tests by student background characteristics

Background characteristic	Language test				
	Malapropism scale − range 0–14	Definition scale + range 5–24	Polysemia scale + range 0–13	Concrete scale − range 0–15	Humanism scale − range 0–9
Type of course					
Philosophy	6.9	13.6	7.1	7.1	5.0
Sociology	7.1	11.7	7.7	6.8	4.7
Mixed	8.6	10.9	6.4	7.0	4.9
Preliminary-year university	9.3	11.1	5.6	8.3	5.4
Preparatory *grandes écoles*	8.0	11.9	7.0	7.0	4.2
Sex					
Males	7.2	12.6	7.2	6.5	4.8
Females	8.3	11.2	6.5	7.6	4.9
Social origin					
Farm-workers	8.1	11.7	6.5	6.8	5.6
Industrial and office-workers	8.0	11.5	6.3	7.0	4.6
Artisans, shopkeepers	8.1	11.0	7.0	7.2	5.0
Middle managers	8.0	11.5	6.7	7.0	4.9
Senior managers	7.4	12.5	7.2	7.0	4.7

Table 1.1   Continued

Background characteristic	Language test				
	Malapropism scale − range 0–14	Definition scale + range 5–24	Polysemia scale + range 0–13	Concrete scale − range 0–15	Humanism scale − range 0–9
Secondary school					
Lycée	7.8	12.3	7.0	6.8	4.8
Collège	8.8	11.5	6.3	7.1	5.2
Private school	7.6	11.0	6.6	6.9	5.0
Secondary curriculum					
Neither Greek nor Latin	8.3	11.4	6.6	6.9	5.2
Latin only	8.1	11.2	6.6	7.0	5.1
Latin and Greek	7.2	12.2	7.3	6.7	4.3
Prior academic success					
Weak	8.2	11.2	6.5	7.3	5.1
Average	7.0	13.1	7.8	6.7	4.7
High	6.1	14.0	8.2	5.7	4.2
Dictionary use					
Very low	7.5	11.5	7.3	6.7	5.2
Low	7.5	12.1	6.8	6.5	4.7
Average	8.2	11.2	6.6	7.3	5.2
High	7.7	14.2	6.8	7.1	4.8
Very high	7.2	11.2	6.7	6.7	4.5
Universities					
Paris	6.6	13.7	7.8	6.9	4.4
Lyon	6.5	13.0	6.5	6.6	5.3
Bordeaux	9.1	10.5	7.5	6.3	4.5
Nancy	8.3	10.5	6.9	7.5	5.2
Dijon	7.1	12.2	6.6	6.8	4.7
Clermont	8.1	11.7	6.8	5.8	5.2
Toulouse	9.3	9.5	6.4	8.6	5.3
Montpellier	8.8	11.4	6.0	7.2	5.0
Caen	7.8	12.5	6.6	6.0	4.3
Lille	9.0	10.7	5.6	6.4	5.3
Rennes	8.3	10.0	7.8	7.6	4.9
Whole sample	8.0	11.6	6.8	6.9	5.0

born into the cultivated classes. Of all the cultural obstacles, those which arise from the language spoken within the setting of the family are unquestionably the most serious and the most insidious. For, especially during the first years of school, comprehension and manipulation of language are the first points of teacher judgement. But the influence of a child's original language setting never ceases to operate. Richness and style of expression are continually taken into account, whether implicitly or explicitly and to different degrees, in all university courses, even scientific ones. Language, however, is not simply a vehicle of thought. Besides a vocabulary more or less rich, it provides a syntax – in other words, a system of categories, more or less complex. The ability to decode and to manipulate complex structures, whether logical or aesthetic, would appear to depend directly on the complexity of the structure of the language first spoken in the family environment, which always passes on some of its features to the language acquired at school. The most important and – from the perspective of the school – the most active part of the cultural heritage, whether general culture or language itself, is thus communicated in the manner of osmosis, even in the absence of any methodical effort or overt action; and this serves only to reinforce the conviction of individuals from cultivated family backgrounds that they owe their learning, their abilities, and their attitudes not to a process of apprenticeship, but to their natural gifts alone.

I Degrees of selection and rates of success

University students have survived the process of scholastic selection to unequal degrees, depending on social origin, sex and type of secondary education. A complete and systematic explanation of how students differ in their knowledge of the language of teaching and in their attitudes towards it needs to take this history of differential selection into account. For those students who have been selected represent very unequal fractions of the original cohorts from which they were drawn. Contrary to appearances, the relationships uncovered by statistical analysis rarely result from the direct, contemporary effect of a particular background variable on differences in measured success. For example, scores on a language test can never be regarded simply as the product of academic background, social origin, sex, or even all these factors acting together. Rather, they reflect the history of each student group, and in particular the differential elimination from the education system that each group has experienced by comparison with other groups having different characteristics. It is thus to commit a fallacy of the form *pars pro toto* to believe that a synchronic analysis, involving a cross-section of students at a given point in time, can directly and exclusively capture the influence of factors like social origin and sex and the interactions between them. For this would imply that the relationships registered at that moment had undergone no change, that they had no past, and were not the product of the continuous action of social and institutional factors over time. In fact, how student background characteristics affect scholastic performance can be fully understood only in the context of the *school career*, which is the sole concrete totality of action.

Degree of selection and social origins

Thus, for example, with working-class children, the first effect of initial inequalities in scholastic language is the elimination of those individuals who have failed to overcome linguistic obstacles or who have been unable to find refuge from the demands of the literary curriculum in an alternative school programme. Those who do reach higher education have had to succeed in a project of acculturation in order to satisfy the irreducible minimum of scholastic demands made on the use of language, and have thus necessarily undergone greater selection than other groups, based on this very criterion.[10] With this minimum standard imposed on every child, the more distant the social group from scholastic language, the higher the rate of scholastic mortality. By the same token, in a population which is the product of selection, unequal selection tends to compensate for the effects of inequality before selection.

By testing those linguistic abilities on which selection in the literary curriculum most directly relies, we are able to capture, at least among middle-class and working-class students, an inversion of the habitually observed relationship between test score and father's occupation. In this inversion, the effects of over-selection experienced by working-class students are only too obvious.[11]

Upper-class students enjoy advantages which are all the more marked outside the cultural domains directly taught and totally controlled by school; for example, as we move from classical theatre to *avant-garde* theatre or from school literature to jazz.[12] So for behaviour like the academic use of academic language, differences in measured performance between social groups will tend to be reduced to the greatest extent, and even reversed. Indeed, it is in this domain that the highly selected students from working-class backgrounds achieve results which are equal to those of their upper-class peers (who are less strongly selected) and better than the results of middle-class students (equally disadvantaged by home language, but less rigorously selected).[13] It appears from a number of indicators that the exceptional abilities and attitudes which have enabled working-class children to reach higher education are due only to a family atmosphere which has proved less unfavourable than that experienced by the great majority of their peers.[14]

Taking this principle to its logical conclusion, the relationship between the hierarchy of results in language ability and the hierarchy of social origins will tend to be progressively reversed as the selection of individuals from disadvantaged backgrounds, and to a lesser extent from the middle classes, becomes more rigorous.[15] Parisian students, for example, obtain better results than provincial students, regardless of social background, but it is among the working classes that this difference is most marked. In Paris, as many as 91 per cent of working-class students obtain high scores (marks over 12), as against only 46 per cent of their class peers in the provinces. By contrast, only 65 per cent of upper-class students from Paris score at this level, and their class peers in the provinces perform almost as well (59 per cent with marks over 12). To understand this reversal of the usual relationship between social background and test success, we need to bear in mind that the cultural atmosphere which goes with living in Paris involves linguistic advantages, on the one hand, but also a particularly rigorous process of selection, on the other.[16] For in Paris the overall level of student performance around which teacher expectations are formed is higher than in the provinces. For each social group we can define the linguistic advantages due to family background and the comparative rigour of access to university as between Paris and the provinces in relative terms (+ or −). To explain the hierarchy of results on the language test, it is enough to combine these values, as in tables 1.2 and 1.3. Our model helps to explain

Table 1.2 Model of linguistic advantages and university selection by social origins and location[a]

Social origins	Location	Linguistic advantages	Selection for university		Linguistic standard
Working classes	Paris	−	++	→	+
	Provinces	− −	+	→	−
Middle classes	Paris	−	+	→	0(+)
	Provinces	− −	0	→	− −
Upper classes	Paris	++	− −	→	0
	Provinces	+	−	→	0

[a] The +'s and −'s define relative values. For the phenomenon in question, the values in the relevant column describe the respective positions of the three social groups, with zero indicating an intermediate location.

Table 1.3 Scores on the definitions test by location and social origins (%)

	Score of 12 or less	Score over 12
Paris		
Working classes	9	91
Middle classes	31	69
Upper classes	35	65
Provinces		
Working classes	54	46
Middle classes	60	40
Upper classes	41	59
Total		
Working classes	46	54
Middle classes	55	45
Upper classes	42.5	57.5

the position of working-class students in Paris by comparison with their class peers in the provinces and also by contrast with upper-class students living in Paris. It also accounts for the relative weakness of middle-class students, who obtain poorer results than working-class students, whether in Paris or in the provinces.

It also follows from this analysis that if the proportion of working-class students reaching university were to increase to any significant degree, the direct correspondence between academic results and social origin would reappear. In higher education, this correspondence can be fully seen only in the domains of learning which are *least* directly controlled by formal schooling; but in secondary education it is evident in the most school-based areas. [17]

Linguistic selection by sex

That girls are able to write much better than boys is a point of stubborn pride among teachers. But when specific kinds of verbal manipulation are measured, male students consistently outperform females. All the language tests in our survey give this result, except for the exercise on the language of humanism. This finding needs to be seen in context. For the situation of women students in universities, in faculties of arts, in particular fields of study, and throughout their school careers varies in a different way in each case from the situation of men.

Girls are condemned to enrolling in arts faculties twice as often as boys.[18] With narrower access to university courses, those who take arts are less selected and less rationally oriented in their choice of studies than male students, just because they are more exposed to this process of relegation. Not surprisingly, their results are poorer. By comparing the gap in language scores for males and females with their respective degrees of selection, our explanatory model, if fully applied, can account for all the empirical data which the most systematic use of multivariate techniques would leave unexplained except by recourse to the notion of 'natural inequalities between the sexes'.

Female students differ as a group from their male counterparts in terms of social background, type of secondary education and scholastic past. For example, 36 per cent of males have received the most classical training [Latin and Greek — trans.] as against only 19.5 per cent of females. Academic success is influenced by all these factors, though to unequal degrees. Multivariate analysis, by controlling for the effects of successive variables, should enable us to examine the net influence of any given variable on linguistic performance in particular subcategories of male and female students, and thus to reveal any interactions underlying the observed relationship between sex and test scores.

How, then, without invoking the myth of natural inequality can we explain the superiority of male students when the gap in performance cannot be attributed to background differences in knowledge of ancient languages, type of secondary school attended, type of secondary studies or social origin? For in each of these various subcategories, test differences between males and females have the same trend, and are generally of the same magnitude.[19] They occur regardless of the type of secondary school attended, except that differences are more marked among graduates from *collèges* (where 62 per cent of males and 35 per cent of females score higher than 12) than *lycées* (where 70 per cent of males and 54 per cent of females achieve these results).

The need to explain achievement differences between female and male students who have reached university is all the more pressing because in the control group drawn from *lycées*, boys and girls obtained more or less equal results.[20] Perhaps this is simply because between these two levels of the education system boys and girls have experienced different degrees of selection. In secondary education, the ratio of male and female students to their respective age-cohorts in the population is very similar.[21] Consequently, boys and girls would appear to be almost equally selected at this level, by contrast with what occurs in arts faculties. For there, and within each social group, female students are very much less strongly selected.

Girls are much more likely than boys to display poor or indifferent levels of skill in the theoretical and abstract manipulation of language which belongs to the very specific requirements of the literary disciplines. This is because the objective mechanisms which condemn girls to arts faculties owe part of their effectiveness to the prevailing social definition of 'feminine' qualities which these mechanisms help to forge. Girls internalize an external necessity which imposes a definition of female studies on them. For an objective destiny to be transmuted into a vocation, and literary studies into the most appropriate female calling, girls and their families need to adhere to the traditional image of feminine qualities, including in particular a sensibility to imponderable nuance and an aptitude for the impressionistic use of language. Even when they enrol in an arts course through deliberate choice or a clearly felt need, their 'choice' still takes into account, if only indirectly, the social destiny which condemns women to a limited range of activities. This relegation will be even less rational or reasonable when it is based on an image of literary studies more attuned to the social stereotype than to the real intellectual demands which define the nature of work in these disciplines.

With one apparent exception, there is nothing which cannot be interpreted in terms of the logic of the relationship between degrees of selection and degrees of success. Male students who took neither Latin nor Greek while in secondary school or who just took Latin obtain better results than females with the same academic background. But among the group of hellenists, it is young women who outshine their male counterparts, with 64 per cent of them, as against 58.5 per cent of males, scoring higher than the median [see table 1.4].

Undoubtedly this reversal of the usual difference is due to the fact that girls have fewer chances than boys of studying both Latin and Greek, so that those who do so are more highly selected than boys with the same training. The traditions which govern curriculum guidance and placement give so little encouragement to girls to enter the most classical stream that the rare few who go against the current would seem to have to satisfy more stringent demands.[22] Similarly, because each relationship acquires its meaning as a function of the overall structure within which it occurs, the most classical training is not linked with greater success in any automatic way. Young women who have done Greek as well as Latin score higher than those who took only Latin or who took neither Greek nor Latin. But the reverse phenomenon is found among young men. Everything again points to the effects of differential selection. Entry to arts courses imposes itself almost as imperatively on boys as on girls when they have taken both Latin and Greek. But boys who took modern subjects or were counselled to take an arts course because of good marks or who made a deliberate choice tended to be more selected than their peers of the same sex.

Table 1.4 Scores on the definitions test by secondary school curriculum and sex (%)[a]

	Score of 12 or less	Score over 12
Neither Greek nor Latin		
Males	34	66
Females	**60**	40
Latin only		
Males	39	61
Females	**58.5**	41.5
Latin and Greek		
Males	**41.5**	48.5
Females	36	**64**
Total		
Males	38	62
Females	**54**	46

[a] Percentages being calculated by columns, the strongest tendency has been set in boldface within each type of secondary school programme.

Comparing linguistic advantages due to family background with rates of access to university and specifically to faculties of arts, the combination of relative values once again explains the hierarchy of results on the definitions test obtained by the different sub-samples of students (see tables 1.5 and 1.6 below).

Degree of selection and type of higher education course

To compare university students by type of course is in fact to rank them according to the severity of selection which they have undergone during secondary school as they were being trained and guided into a programme of studies more or less esteemed by the system of higher education. And indeed, as we ascend the hierarchy, which ranges from courses with a mixed combination of subjects to specializations in sociology and then philosophy, or from the preliminary year in a university to a preparatory class for a *grande école littéraire*, the results on our linguistic test rise in regular fashion from the freest courses to the most canonical disciplines.

Located at the same formal level of study, preliminary-year students at university and preparatory students for the *grandes écoles* obtain very different results. In the test on identifying malapropisms, for example, nearly 60 per

Table 1.5 Model of linguistic advantages, university and arts faculty selection by social origins and sex

Social origins and sex	Linguistic advantages	Selection for university	Selection for arts faculty		Linguistic standard
Working classes					
Males	−	+	+	→	+
Females	−	+ +	− −	→	−
Middle classes					
Males	−	0	+	→	0
Females	−	0	−	→	− −
Upper classes					
Males	+ +	− −	+ +	→	+ +
Females	+ +	− −	−	→	−

Expressing relative degrees of selection in algebraic terms (+, −) gives an approximate translation of the chances of access to university of different sub-groups and of their conditional probabilities of enrolling in arts faculties (see P. Bourdieu and J.-C. Passeron, *Les Héritiers*, pp. 15−16).

Table 1.6 Scores on the definitions test by social origins and sex (%)

	Score of 12 or less	Score over 12
Working classes		
Males	35.5	64.5
Females	53.5	46.5
Middle classes		
Males	43	57
Females	60.5	39.5
Upper classes		
Males	33	67
Females	47	53
Total		
Males	38	62
Females	54	46

cent of the most selected and longest-schooled group commit fewer than nine errors, as against only 30 per cent of the preliminary-year university students.

Traditionalists make much of the 'difference in standard' between students preparing for the *grandes écoles* and preliminary-year university students. But before attributing this difference to irreducible inequalities of gifts which result in the best students being sent to the cultural paradise of noble studies and the studious plebs to the purgatory of 'mass education', we should stop to examine the social characteristics of these two groups whose academic destinies are so different. Young people from senior- and middle-management backgrounds make up 57 per cent and 26 per cent respectively of students preparing for the *grandes écoles*, and 38 per cent and 37 per cent of preliminary-year university students. Moreover, among preparatory students, 38 per cent have done Latin and Greek, as against only 16 per cent of their counterparts at university, a difference which is linked to social origins. Students preparing for the *grandes écoles* are all younger than 21, but this is true of only 80 per cent of the university sample. Finally, it is from the *lycées* that the preparatory students come in the overwhelming majority of cases (89.5 per cent), compared to just 60 per cent for preliminary-year students. Young people preparing for the *grandes écoles* are the elite in whom our school system takes great pride. The superiority of their results proves yet again that the language test, and especially the definitions test, adequately measures what we hoped it would: namely, the range of linguistic behaviours required by literary examinations. Our decision to measure the value judgements of the teacher by adopting his own criteria of judgement thus succeeds as an approach, without implying any judgement as such on the value of these criteria.

There is a complete divergence of results on the definitions test between students preparing for the *grandes écoles* and their peers at university. All the preparatory students score above a threshold representing the standard that French higher education demands of those it admits to its 'elite' streams.[23] If 74 per cent of preliminary-year students and 65 per cent of preparatory students score around the average level of performance (between 9 and 13 points), 14 per cent of the university group score below 9, but not a single student from the preparatory-class group is found in this region. Moreover, of the group preparing for the *grandes écoles*, 34 per cent score over 13, as against 10 per cent at university (see appendix 3).

Turning to the test on multiple meanings (polysemia), results for students in the *classes préparatoires* and those in the *année propédeutique* at university again diverge sharply. On this test, the respective modes of performance vary from 5 to 7 and the medians from 5.6 to 7. However, scores for each group tend to be normally distributed, rather than skewed, as in the case of the definitions test. Given that the exercise on multiple meanings also related to the language of ideas and appealed to a learned, analytical attitude, it is striking that it does not discriminate between preparatory students and preliminary-year university students in the same way as the definitions test. We may well wonder about the traditional system of academic marking (most closely linked to the definitions test), one of whose consequences is to accentuate differences in standards of attainment. For while we believe that we are assigning marks according to a well-calibrated scale of performance, in practice we are content with dividing candidates into three broad categories of 'brilliant', 'mediocre', and 'worthless'.[24] The type of coding applied by the examiner illustrates the specific effect of *academic* marking. Marks are used to express judgements which are at once total, categorical and subtle. Beneath the fine-grained differences of half-points and quarter-points sought out and produced by the marker, there operates a basic division of candidates into broad groups, within which the hierarchies of performance are in fact poorly defined. Studies of the behaviour of examiners show that fluctuations in marks across multiple corrections occur inside certain intervals. These class intervals correspond to qualitative categories of teacher judgement, which a numerical score denotes in a variable way. Below 5 out of 20, an assignment is deemed 'worthless', and usually attracts derision or indignation. Between 6 and 8, it is 'mediocre' or 'depressing'. Between 9 and 11 – or 'around the mean', as we say – sulky resignation is the reaction (acquiescence even in disapproval); from 12 to 15, lavishings of encouragement; and beyond this, 'brilliant'.

Turning to results within the sample of university students, a similar hierarchical pattern can be seen, but this time by academic discipline. Students who are doing a mixed group of subjects always have the weakest scores on the three most academic tests.[25] But this gap in performance disappears when it comes to knowledge of technical language and knowledge of the language of humanism. Sociology students obtain slightly better results, but are consistently weaker than philosophy students. This difference also disappears in the domains of technical language and the language of humanism. The 'freest' courses recruit young people who are least well-adapted to academic demands, and the more or less large proportion of places which these least selected students occupy by way of refuge thus gives expression to the institutional hierarchy among university courses, while at the same time contributing to its perpetuation.[26]

Sociology students tend to be older than other student groups.[27] They more often come from private schools,[28] and, having more often done Latin,[29] have not been trained for science courses. These characteristics suggest that many of them have marked time at university before embarking on a new direction, whether profitably or otherwise. Mixed courses recruit a

high proportion of young women who are just starting out on their studies
– 70 per cent as against 58 per cent among philosophy students and only
51.5 per cent among sociology students. They are younger than sociology
students, and seem to be 'trying out' various subjects. Undoubtedly we
would expect to find poorly chosen vocations in this group, often ending in
interrupted studies.

Philosophy students in general achieve results which are clearly superior
to those of sociology students; 75 per cent, as against 53 per cent, score
over 12 on the definitions test. Multivariate analysis shows that it is
among philosophy students that the class advantage of an upper-class over a
working-class background is greatest, while among sociology students it is
actually *reversed*. A discipline like sociology thus tends to play the role of
sheltering young people from senior-management families whose adaptation
to academic demands has been poorest. The same tendency is found among
middle-class students, though to a lesser extent. Doing philosophy means
performing better than when doing sociology. This divergence in scores
between philosophy and sociology is lowest of all among working-class
students [see table 1.7].

Similarly, in each type of course male students as a group obtain better

Table 1.7   Scores on the definitions test by type of course
and social origins (%)

	Score of 12 or less	Score over 12
Philosophy		
Working classes	25.5	74.5
Middle classes	34.5	65.5
Upper classes	20	80
Sociology		
Working classes	33.5	66.5
Middle classes	46	54
Upper classes	53	47
Mixed courses		
Working classes	60	40
Middle classes	66	34
Upper classes	51	49
Total		
Working classes	46	54
Middle classes	55	45
Upper classes	42.5	57.5

results than females, but the difference is greatest in philosophy. In other words, male superiority is even more marked in those disciplines in which the performance of all students is higher; in philosophy the gap is 20.5 per cent, in sociology 12 per cent, and among the dilettantes 8.5 per cent. This finding appears to support the view that the respective proportions of male and female students whose higher education vocations are poorly thought out vary according to academic discipline. Philosophy is the discipline in which the number of males who are most rationally oriented in their choice of studies also most clearly surpasses the corresponding number of females. The more marginal disciplines, where overall test results for both males and females are weaker, attract fewer male choices, and this tends to reduce attainment differences between the sexes.

* * *

If all the observed variations in language ability proceed from a single source which has different effects depending on the total system of relationships within which and through which it operates, this is because they are the expression not of a series of partial connections, but of a structure in which it is the complete system of relationships which determines the meaning of any particular association. Multivariate analysis, in this context, plays only a heuristic role. Endless problems of interpretation would arise – or indeed, a reification of purely abstract associations – if, under our explanatory approach, the action of the real historical structure did not restore to the merely logical wholes partitioned by analytical criteria the life of the social groups as distinguished by the totality of their relationships with the past and through this historical mediation with the present.

II Scholastic past as mediation

To completely unravel the various associations between social background and test results, we thus need to turn to the relationships between scholastic past and success in each social group. Indeed, it is through all the components of a *school career* as a whole – choice of curriculum stream or of programme, type of school attended, and previous success – that the direct influence of family background is relayed by being translated into a properly scholastic logic.

Significant associations between the variables so far employed in our analysis and academic results appear only in the most scholastic of the language tests. However, an index of *prior academic success*, based on the number of honours obtained in previous examinations, and *knowledge of*

Latin and Greek are more strongly linked to high rates of performance on the language tests (regardless of the particular test) than all other background factors.

Degree of success and knowledge of Greek and Latin

Given the present framework of teaching traditions and practices, a greater mastery of language always appears among students who have taken ancient languages. We might well accept that classical training gives students superior facility with language through the discipline of a privileged mental and linguistic apprenticeship. But this relationship may conceal other, more fundamental links, and we need to examine whether classical training acts in fact as a mediation through which other factors exert their influence. Under the present regime of recruitment to the various curriculum streams in secondary school, Latin and Greek are taken mainly by children who have distinguished themselves by a much stronger conformity to scholastic demands. In our study this includes a proportion of the small group of already over-selected working-class students (24.5 per cent), which is almost as high as is found among their peers from well-to-do backgrounds (28 per cent) who have all the means at their disposal for transmuting social privilege into scholastic privilege.

But there are other reasons for doubting the virtues which pedagogical conservatism attributes to classical training. How can we explain, for example, that it is only the *most* classical training (Latin *and* Greek) which is linked with the best scores, regardless of test, while knowledge of Latin alone confers no advantage over modern subjects? The tests which are best designed to measure the ability in mental gymnastics which apprenticeship in Latin is supposed to develop — recognizing multiple meanings (polysemia) and malapropisms, or 'false meanings' (as examiners call them) — reveal no significant inequality in performance between Latinists and others. It is only students who have taken both Latin and Greek who are distinguished by their verbal ease, because it is they who were self-selected (or were selected) in terms of the image of a hierarchy of curriculum streams in which classical studies occupies the pinnacle. In the very first years of secondary school, they had to exhibit a particular degree of success in order to claim entry to a stream which the system reserves to its elite. And indeed, it is also to this stream that those teachers gravitate who are most apt at turning good pupils into the best pupils.[30]

Knowledge of Greek and Latin may thus be associated with greater success; but this does not mean that success is due to their particular educational virtues as such.[31] If the students in medicine who obtain the best results are those who have done Greek, the hellenists also contribute a large proportion of the worst results.[32]

These findings do not decide unequivocally between different teaching choices. Having demonstrated a relationship between the most classical studies in secondary school and test scores, we can draw, indifferently, one of two conclusions. Either this training gives a technical preparation for the comprehension and manipulation of the language of ideas, which in turn is a precondition for success in the most abstract studies, so that training in Latin and Greek should be generalized. Or it is appropriate to relax, if not abandon, the linguistic requirements of secondary education so that academic success ceases to depend on an old-fashioned programme of intellectual training. Success in the present examination system is favoured by a particular group of studies; so we can argue, in other words, either in favour of this training or against the examination regime which continues to require it.[33]

From social past to scholastic past

Familiarity with the language of ideas remains an essential factor in academic success, and this is understandable once we recognize the weight attached to rhetorical ease by the implicit or explicit criteria of the examination system. Students who have taken Latin and Greek score highest on the language tests; their superiority is linked with high levels of attainment in school; and they have achieved the best results in previous examinations.[34] Selected by and for their rhetorical ease, they thus most completely fulfil the image of the conforming student which examinations in their French form demand and bring into existence through this very demand.

To fully understand how students from different social backgrounds relate to the world of culture and, more precisely, to the institution of schooling, we need to recapture the logic through which the conversion of social heritage into scholastic heritage operates in different class situations.[35] At the same time, however, we should not lose sight of the fact that there are ways in which each situation can be differentiated by secondary factors, and that these may promote different relationships to the same underlying situation and to the cultural atmosphere which typically accompanies it, thus transforming or even reversing the effects of social class.

For example, the test scores of young people from senior-management backgrounds tend to be distributed in a bimodal fashion (and other cultural behaviours also display this dual tendency).[36] This statistical category in fact conceals two populations, which differ markedly in their cultural orientations and also, no doubt, in their secondary social characteristics.[37] Those who have academically exploited their cultural capital stand out from those whose privileged circumstances have kept them at school simply out of habit. Attendance at a *lycée* is a good indicator of the seriousness and success with which studies are pursued. Of students from a senior-management background who attended a *lycée*, 64.5 per cent scored more than 12 on the definitions test. By comparison, only 47 per cent of their counterparts who went to a private school did as well.[38]

The diversity of young people from senior-management families appears even more clearly from the pattern of their results on the definitions test. The distinctly bimodal spread of their results contrasts with the results of working-class and middle-class students, which present a more regular trend. Scores on the language of humanism test display a different social pattern. Average performance shifts upwards in line with class position, but within each social group the distribution tends to be normal. This test demands only a knowledge of lexis (by contrast with the definitions test), and it is doubtless because of this that success depends more directly and more automatically on the inheritance of cultural advantages rather than their active utilization [see table 1.8].

Disadvantages due to social background are mainly relayed through curriculum guidance and placement.[39] It is therefore only to be expected

Table 1.8 Scores on the definitions test by secondary school curriculum and social origins (%)

	Score of 12 or less	Score over 12
Neither Greek nor Latin		
Working classes	52	48
Middle classes	54	46
Upper classes	39	61
Latin only		
Working classes	48	52
Middle classes	58	42
Upper classes	52	48
Latin and Greek		
Working classes	38.5	61.5
Middle classes	55	45
Upper classes	26.5	73.5
Total		
Working classes	46	54
Middle classes	55	45
Upper classes	42.5	57.5

that young people from senior-management families will obtain better results when they have received the most classical training or the least classical. By contrast, working-class children excel in the group of Latinists because their choice of Latin is undoubtedly due to particular features of their family background. Belonging to a social category in which the likelihood of being placed in a Latin class is rarer, they have had to display particular qualities to be rewarded with this placement and to persevere with it.[40] An analogous phenomenon can be seen in the case of working-class students who took the full classical programme of Latin and Greek. They achieve results which are almost equal to the scores for all students with this same academic history (61.5 per cent, as against 62 per cent for the whole group). Their poorer showing by contrast with upper-class students (73.5 per cent) can be explained by the fact that they are being compared with the fraction of well-off students who have fully utilized their privileges and who have completely exploited their position within the curriculum, thanks to the great many advantages associated with a cultivated background.

* * *

It would be imprudent to claim to have isolated the determining factors underlying the system of relationships made up by scholastic careers and, *a fortiori*, a single governing factor. Success at the highest level of the curriculum still remains very closely linked to the most distant scholastic past, and through this to social origins. Access to higher education, and even attainment at this level, are strongly related to success during the first years of school. What the results of our study suggest is that very early choices, such as admission to a more or less classical stream, are connected with very high chances of access to higher education and to success in it. In short, the game is over early, if indeed we can still speak of a game when the chances of winning are so unequally apportioned among children from different social backgrounds.

But we should not see in social background simply the first link in a chain of causal connections. On the contrary, it is wholly in each of its mediations that class asserts its influence. Only by abstraction can we refer, for example, to 'the student' or to the student child of the worker or even (as in multivariate analysis) to the student child born of working-class parents and taking Latin or Greek. From the situation of a working-class child, we may be able to understand what it means to him to be studying Latin or not studying it, to be attending a teachers' college or a *petit séminaire*, to become a philosophy teacher or an experimental psychologist. But we cannot reassemble this or that experience from whichever one happens to be taken as the key to the whole. The real experiences described by these abstractions assume concrete, unitary and meaningful form only thanks to the fact that they are constituted by the class situation, the point from which every possible view unfolds and upon which no single point of view is possible.

APPENDIX 1   CHARACTERISTICS OF THE SAMPLE

As in the preceding surveys, the questionnaire was administered to groups of students who were actually attending lectures in arts faculties. However, these groups are in general a close enough reflection of the arts faculty population. While the sample comprised 63.6% females, B.U.S. statistics for 1961–2 give 63.3%. The breakdown of the sample according to father's occupation is also near enough to B.U.S. statistics. Thus 28% of the sample was drawn from working-class backgrounds (farm-workers, industrial workers, office-workers), 19% from artisans and shopkeepers, 16.9% from middle management and 36.1% from the upper classes. According to B.U.S. statistics, the respective proportions in the faculty population are 20.8%, 13.6%, 23% and 30.4%, the categories of rentiers and others accounting for 12.2% of the population.

Turning to differences between male and female students, the age-pattern observed in previous surveys was found once again: women are younger than men at any given level of studies, with 45.9% being under 21, compared to only 26.7% of men. On the other hand, a larger proportion of women are from well-to-do

Table 1 Social background by university (frequencies)

University	Working classes[a] (n = 139)	Middle classes[b] (n = 178)	Upper classes[c] (n = 179)	Total (n = 496)
Bordeaux	4	10	13	27
Caen	17	11	9	37
Clermont	4	8	6	18
Dijon	9	1	7	17
Lille	6	10	5	21
Lyon	13	16	18	47
Montpellier	26	35	21	82
Nancy	7	14	16	37
Paris	23	32	60	115
Rennes	11	21	5	37
Toulouse	19	20	19	58

[a] Farm-workers, industrial workers, office-workers.
[b] Artisans, shopkeepers, middle managers.
[c] Senior managers, liberal professions.

backgrounds, with 38.3% and 18.1% coming respectively from senior- and middle-management levels, as against 35.5% and 14% of men.

On social origin, the trends reported in previous surveys were confirmed. Thus, upper-class students are younger than their counterparts from farm-worker and industrial-worker backgrounds; 45% of the children of senior managers are less than 21 years old, as against 34.5% of working-class students.

The control groups from final-year *lycée* classes (philosophy and advanced mathematics) comprised several classes from Paris and the provinces – in Paris a class of boys and three classes of girls, in suburban Paris three classes from different *lycées*, and in the provinces a co-educational class, giving an overall total of 306 pupils.

The preceding remarks concerning differences between boys and girls at the faculty level apply equally well to the *lycées*. Thus 41.5% of girls were less than 18, as against 27.5% of boys, and 58% of girls were from senior-management backgrounds, as against 42% of boys.

APPENDIX 2   THE QUESTIONNAIRE

Centre de sociologie Européenne
10, rue Monsieur-le-Prince
Paris 6

Sociology of Education

1 Nationality . . . .   2 University . . . .

3 Sex . . . .   4 Age . . . .

5 Certificates taken . . . .

6 Number of years at university (preliminary year included) . . . .

7 Father's occupation (specific details) . . . .
Paternal grandfather's occupation . . . .

8 Did you receive your secondary education in: – a public *lycée* – a public *collège* – a private school?

9 In the course of your secondary education, did you study: Greek? Latin?

10 What grade did you receive at the following examinations? Mark the relevant cell with a cross:

	Pass	Satisfactory	Good	Very good
Baccalauréat, 1st stage				
Baccalauréat, 2nd stage				
Preliminary-year exam				

11   In which of the following sections did you complete the second stage of
     your *baccalauréat?*

     − Philosophy
     − Advanced mathematics
     − Experimental sciences
     − Technical

12   Do you have a French dictionary in your home? Yes. No. Which one?

13   How often do you consult dictionaries in a library? Never − very excep-
     tionally − rarely − sometimes − often.

14   Name the dictionaries which you have consulted most often?............

15   When, in the course of your reading, you encounter a little-known or
     unknown word, are you in the habit of looking it up or confirming its
     meaning in a dictionary? Yes. No.

16   If, in the course of a lecture, you hear one or several words which you are
     not familiar with or don't know at all, would you normally make a note of
     them and check their meaning in a dictionary? Yes. No.

17   In your opinion, what working tools are indispensable for good writing?...

Test 1

Below you will find a series of sentences. In each one you should underline the
words which seem to you to be employed incorrectly (poetic licence and other
artistic conventions are excluded).

Some sentences may not contain any term incorrectly used; others may contain
several.

Do not try to discuss the statements made in the sentences; just look for words
incorrectly used or confused with others.

Here is an example: 'Modern science proves that phenomena are governed by a
dangerous (*hasardeux*) determinism.'

The test is not concerned with what modern science may or may not prove, but
only with recognizing that the word 'dangerous' is out of place here. In fact, the
word signifies either 'presence of risk, peril or danger' or 'freely inviting peril'. But
'hazardous' is not linked with the scientific sense of the word 'chance' (*hasard*), and
thus could in no way signify 'statistical' or 'probabilistic'.

1   The generic sanctions provided by ancient legislations against *incunable
    debtors were diverse but always very severe.[41]

2   Beauty is very difficult to appraise objectively; still, *teratology endlessly
    passes value judgements upon works of art. As a result there is a generalized
    impartiality on the part of the public towards axiological problems.

3 The ennobling of commoners was performed not just by the English monarchy.

4 Taken in its etymological acceptance (*acceptation*) the term 'alienation' has a clear and numinous (*numineux*) sense; unfortunately the inconsiderate (*inconsidéré*) use made of it today has very much obscured it.

5 Formal logic represents one of the first systematic efforts to make an inventory of the kinds of compatibility and incompatibility between propositions. It teaches us, e.g., that we cannot at the same time affirm 'All As are B' and 'Some As are not B', for this would be to simultaneously affirm two contrary propositions.

6 The sequence of axioms flowing from one another deductively, mathematical reasoning is no less apodeictic than the Aristotelian syllogism.

7 Belief in a transcendental god is at the centre of a soteriological religion like Christianity.

8 The creation of a vernacular language – as it was hoped Esperanto would be – is sometimes considered the *prodrome of better international understanding.

9 The civil law is the palladium of property.

10 When the existence of evil is not justified by a theodicy, the collateral security (*nantissement*) of the privileged classes in the midst of general misery strikes everyone as a virtual scandal.

11 Causal imputation is, in history, such an uncertain and dubitative course that it is often necessary to be content with pure conjunctures (*conjonctures*).

12 It would scarcely be serious to explain by the levelling (*égalitaire*) stratification of African societies that the productivity of Africa in coal reaches only 30,000 tonnes per year. But is the explanation by climacteric (*climatériques*) influences more plausible?

13 Freud put forward hypotheses on the aetiology of neuroses which are still discussed today. In any case, no neuropath can completely ignore them in his therapeutic work.

Test 2

Define the following terms as rigorously as you can:

- Antinomy
- Cadastral

- Epistemology
- Extension (of a concept)
- Manichaeism

Test 3

Enumerate all the possible meanings of each of the words below:

Example: *Charge.*

1 The load a man can carry.
2 Charge for a firearm.
3 Quantity of electricity.
4 Charge of a troop.
5 Roll of a drum.
6 Onerous obligation.
7 Public duty.
8 Presumption of guilt.
9 Caricature.

Attribute
Function
Image
Participation
Realism

Test 4

Here is a list of words. Following each of them you will find six other words. Underline which of these six has the same meaning as the original word (or is very close to it).

N.B. There is never only one word in each list which may be considered a synonym, but there is invariably at least one.

Stumble: stop, catch, disapprove, trip, lecture someone, join.

Layout: gallery, temple, garden, approaches, arrangement, hinge-pins.

Quarrier: carrier, paver, singer, quarry-worker, tile-layer, leveller.

Disposition: terminology, regeneration, diagram, complexity, temperament, organism.

Combe: dale, promontory, gulf, summit, mountain, resting place.

Supernumeracy: extra, reservist, defendant, steward, accessary, initiate.

Emetic: unguent, vomitive, sedative, perfume, drier, enamel.

Fuliginous: serrated, jagged, contradictory, inconsistent, containing soot, containing fatty elements.

Funambulist: absent-minded, acrobat, tight-rope dancer, original, somnambulist, practical-joker.

Girandole: merry-go-round, chandelier, oliphant, megalith, garland. [Only five words given — trans.]

Interpolate: specify, intercalate, invert, transgress, challenge, change.

Permissible: rare, vacationist, allowed, recommended, orderly, indifferent.

Marasmus: regression, difficulty, liveliness, remorse, wasting, worry.

Miasma: serosity, effluvium, odour, polyp, pimple, infiltration.

Sea-green: dark blue, penetrating, indeterminate, strabismic, light green, changing.

Pier: flute, cap, fronton, mortar-board, small trowel, between bays.

Now, here are a number of terms followed by four definitions. Of the four, only one fits.

Broaching
- is the operation which consists in regularizing the internal diameter of a tube or hole.
- is the operation which consists in fining down a metal plate.
- is the operation which consists in de-oxidizing a metallic surface.
- is the operation which consists in polishing a finished metal piece.

Milling
- is the operation which consists in the circular polishing of two surfaces.
- is the operation which consists in producing a helicoidal track in the interior of a hole.
- is the laundering process which consists in putting a starched collar into shape.
- is the operation which consists in widening a hole bored in metal or wood.

Fallow
- is a field in which legumes are planted.
- is the agricultural technique which consists in alternating crops on the same land.
- is the condition of land periodically left idle.
- is common land open to the flocks of all the villagers.

Jointer
- is a large compass.
- is a file for precious metals.
- is a planing tool.
- is a gimlet with a large diameter.

Test 5

Instructions are the same as for the preceding exercise: for each of the following terms underline the exact definition:

Counterpoint

- is a type of musical composition which favours consonances at the expense of melodic continuity.
- is the musical technique whose object is the co-ordination of simultaneous sounds (or chords).
- is the musical technique whose object is the superimposition of several melodic lines.
- is the technique of composition in which sounds are produced on the upbeat or upon the unaccented position in the bar.

A sonata

- is a piece of instrumental music made up of several parts in different movements.
- is a musical piece in which only a small number of instruments appear.
- is a piece of music in which only keyboard instruments are used.
- is a piece of instrumental music in which a part for voice is introduced.

Scumble

- is a painted surface perfectly levelled.
- is a painting executed with a single coat of paint.
- is the application of a coat of transparent paint over a coat of opaque paint.
- is the effect obtained by excluding from the palette colours which risk absorbing light.

A sanguine

- is a drawing done on red or ochre paper.
- is a drawing done with haematite crayon.
- is a painting in which red tones dominate.
- is a sketch of a nude.

Helen

- was the niece of Agamemnon.
- was the sister of Clytemnestra.
- was the daughter of Agamemnon.
- was the daughter of the king of Crete.

A litotes

- is a figure in rhetoric which consists in ironically saying the contrary of what one would wish to have understood.
- is the use of a brief or direct expression.
- is the rhetorical figure which consists in using an expression which says less so as to have more understood.

    – is an error of reasoning which consists in implicitly introducing the term to be defined in the definition given.

Proteus

    – was a demigod against whom Heracles fought.
    – was the father of Achilles.
    – was a legendary animal which was impossible to catch.
    – was a sea-god.

Stagirite

    – is the surname of a philosopher.
    – is the surname of an ascetic monk.
    – is the surname of a general from the hellenistic era.
    – is the name of a celebrated sophism.

Seide

    – is the name of a biblical character.
    – is the name of a Muslim character in a tragedy of Voltaire.
    – is the name of one of the heroes in the *Thousand and One Nights*.
    – is the surname of a courtier under Louis XIV.

Did you find this test: Very easy – easy – average – difficult – very difficult?

APPENDIX 3   TEST RESULTS BY TYPE OF COURSE AND SOCIAL ORIGIN

1 Results by type of course

On all the tests, preliminary-year university students obtain weaker results than students in the preparatory classes for the *grandes écoles*. In those tests which are scaled according to the number of *errors* – identification of malapropisms, technical language, language of humanism – the mode always favours students in the preparatory classes. In the definitions test (scored positively), the distribution of the preparatory students' results (which are higher overall) deviates completely from normality, and is skewed positively – i.e., on the side of the poorest performance. In the test on identifying multiple meanings (polysemia) – scored positively – the modal mark definitely displays the superiority of students in the preparatory classes of the *grandes écoles*.

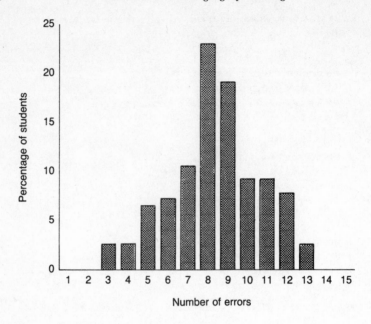

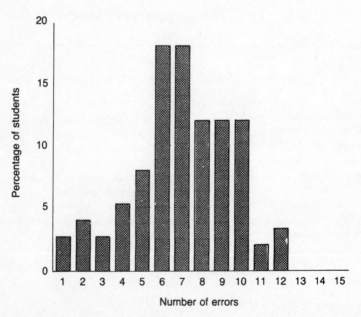

Figure 1 Malapropism test: results for preliminary-year university students (*above*),
preparatory *grande école* students (*below*).

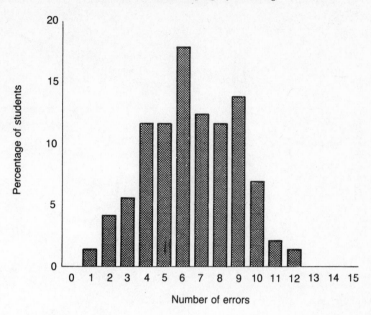

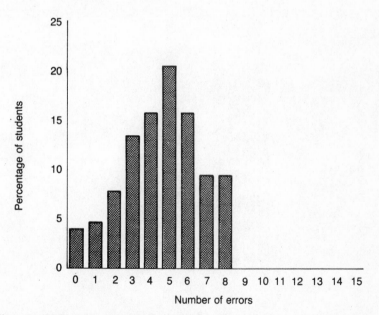

Figure 2 Technical language test: results for preliminary-year university students (*above*), preparatory *grande école* students (*below*).

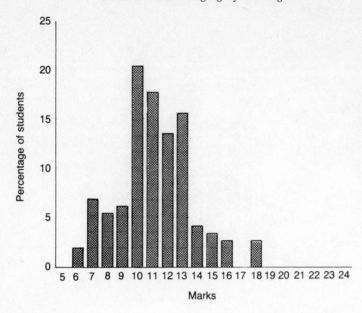

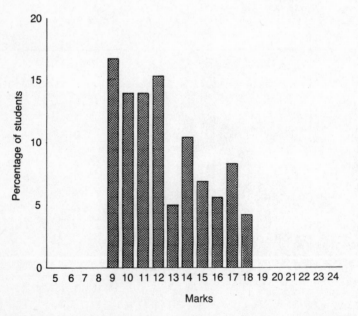

Figure 3 Definitions test: results for preliminary-year university students (*above*), preparatory *grande école* students (*below*).

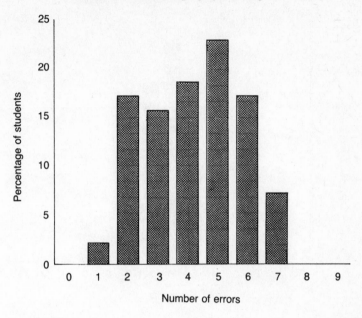

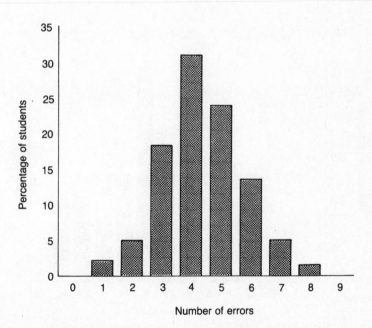

Figure 4 Language of humanism test: results for preliminary-year university students (*above*), preparatory *grande école* students (*below*).

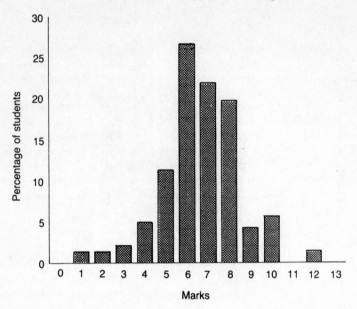

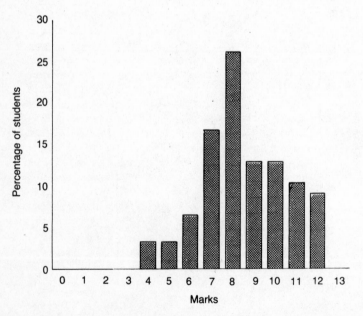

Figure 5 Multiple meanings (polysemia) test: results for preliminary-year university students (*above*), preparatory *grande école* students (*below*).

2   *Results by social origin (students preparing the* licence*)*

If a simple reading of medians (cf. pp. 38–9) makes the superiority of the children of senior managers over all other groups quite evident – and also the weakness of middle-class students – examination of the distribution shows that this central tendency conceals important within-group differences. Thus, on the definitions test, the distribution of results for senior-management backgrounds is distinctly bimodal, which testifies once again to the fact that there are two possible utilizations of cultural heritage. For the test on the language of humanism (marked negatively), the histograms show that the proportion of students lying within the zone of the best results (on the left of the graph) rises as we climb the social hierarchy, since 32.8% of working-class students, 35.4% of middle-class students and 46.3% of upper-class students made fewer than five errors. But the three distributions are normal.

APPENDIX 4   LEXICOLOGICAL ANALYSIS OF LECTURES

The survey instrument was designed to test student comprehension of terms which were characteristic not only of the language of teaching, but of the fiction which assumes that such words are known. Consequently, in choosing terms for inclusion in the test, we did not work exclusively and mechanically according to the rule of the frequency with which words appeared in lectures. Leaving aside the fact that the analysis of the frequency of words in a lecture does not isolate, *ipso facto*, the specific lexis through which a lecture is linked with an idiomatic use of language, certain terms whose frequency of appearance was relatively weak illustrated perfectly well – to the extent that they were introduced without definition or commentary – the type of linguistic demand peculiar to higher education. Thus terms will be found in the language tests which occur with differing degrees of frequency in the six lectures on philosophy and on sociology given at Lille and Paris that were analysed.

Among the high-frequency terms – i.e., those which appeared from 5 to 20 times in a one-hour lecture – we have excluded terms such as 'society', 'sociology', 'culture', 'philosophy', 'history', 'laws' or 'structure' which, through the multiplicity or even the imprecision of their meanings, did not lend themselves to the intended linguistic tests. On the other hand, we have retained from the sociology lectures the terms 'function', 'stratification' and 'conjuncture'; from the philosophy lectures 'antimony' and 'epistemology'; and from the language common to both 'contrary', 'virtual', 'generic', 'participation', 'image' and 'realism'.

Among the terms whose frequency was lowest and which only appeared once in the lectures we analysed, we have retained – because they were followed by no explanation – the terms 'Manichaeism', 'extension', 'attribute', 'apodeictic', 'transcendental', 'valorize', 'acceptance', 'axiom', 'dubitative', 'productivity' and 'disinterestedness'.

Among the numerous difficult terms which appeared only once or twice, we have kept the terms 'cadastral', 'numinous', 'neuropath', 'climacteric', 'incunable',

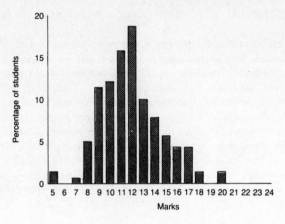

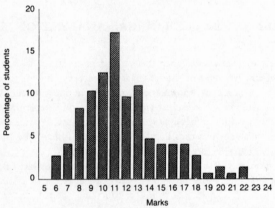

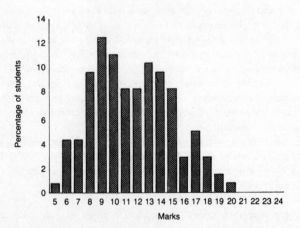

Figure 6 Definitions test: results for working-class students (*top*), middle-class students (*middle*), and upper-class students (*bottom*).

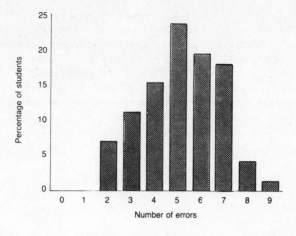

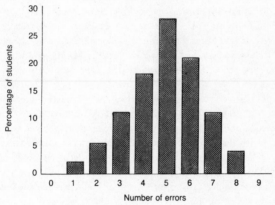

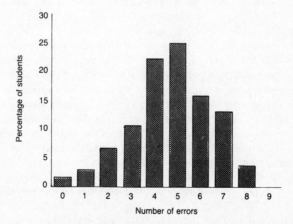

Figure 7 Language of humanism test: results for working-class students (*top*), middle-class students (*middle*) and upper-class students (*bottom*).

'vernacular', 'teratology', 'ennobling', 'collateral security' (*nantissement*), 'soteriology' – terms which, despite their technicality, were introduced without the least definition.

This method concerns only the first three tests intended to measure comprehension of the language of teaching properly speaking. The test intended to measure the comprehension of concrete language constitutes an enrichment of the Pichois test. We have added terms from agricultural and industrial technology to contrast it more clearly with the other tests. The last test selected technical terms from the language of the arts or proper names from the classical humanities occurring in manuals or extracts selected for secondary school.

NOTES

1   The survey involved a range of student audiences in French universities (see appendix 1), following previous surveys by the Centre de sociologie Européenne. See P. Bourdieu and J.-C. Passeron, *Les Étudiants et leurs études*, Cahiers du Centre de sociologie Européenne, no. 1 (Mouton, Paris and The Hague, 1964).

2   The pilot study was conducted by P. Bourdieu, M. Maget and J.-C. Passeron. See Ronéo-typé report from the Centre de sociologie Européenne, July 1961.

3   Were we, despite everything, to contest the sample's representativeness according to academic discipline, the global findings (e.g., on the degree of misunderstanding) would remain rigorously incontestable in the case of sociology students and also students in ethics and sociology; for in respect of these groups the sample constituted a true census. The sample was drawn from students in sociology and in ethics and sociology in the faculties at Bordeaux, Caen, Clermont, Dijon, Lille, Lyon, Montpellier, Nancy, Paris, Rennes and Toulouse. For the purpose of comparison, on the other hand, the sample was extended to a number of control groups: students from a range of disciplines in arts faculties, a preparatory class for a *grande école littéraire* and several final-year classes in *lycées* in Paris and the provinces. In appendix 1, details will be found regarding the breakdown of the sample.

4   This is why the distribution of results often exhibits a tendency towards skewness (cf. histograms, appendix 3). Given the difficulty of these tests for the students – a difficulty which results from the deliberate decision to relate student performance to pre-established norms and not to norms established *a posteriori* as a function of the results – oscillations around the mean are not free. The principle of arrest (*mécanisme d'arrêt*) is here always situated on the side of weak performance (that is to say, on the side of the maximum number of errors or the weakest positive mark), because the central tendency of the distribution skews the greatest number of students in this direction. In view of the trend of most of the distributions, we have compared groups and subgroups using the median and the inter-quartile range as measures of central tendency and dispersion.

5   This concerned terms used with high frequency, such as 'epistemology', 'modality', 'specific', 'plausible', and 'participation'.

6 We may be forgiven for using the term 'malapropism' [accepted in English – trans.] to denote errors committed by students in their knowledge of terms used 'out of place'. Mr E. Weil, professor of philosophy in the Faculty of Arts at Lille, who suggested this exercise to us, drew our attention to one of Sheridan's characters, Mrs Malaprop, whose name and errors of language might justify this neologism.

7 The findings of this test of misunderstanding in communication would appear to remain valid *a minimis*, since terms used with very high frequency are eliminated when they belong exclusively to the idiom of one teacher.

8 See appendix 4, where details of the method employed for lexicological analysis will be found.

9 We have been led to distinguish two groups of tests which can be characterized, *grosso modo*, as more or less academic. As much by their lexicological content as by the mental posture which they presuppose, the tests on identifying 'malapropisms', on definitions and on identifying words with multiple meanings (polysemia) are those which most closely meet the requirements of academic practice. The remaining tests, by contrast, question either an extended knowledge of the lexis or a more liberal culture. The definitions test is particularly critical, since the principle of marking was nearest to the one which guides a teacher in the correction of examination scripts; it will be seen that this is precisely the test in which the role of the different factors of inequality becomes most apparent. And this conclusion is valid, *a fortiori*, for actual teacher judgement; for the marking of the test has been carried out under conditions which minimize subjectivity of judgement: involvement of several judges and list of explicit criteria for the attribution of marks (from 1 to 5). See below, n. 22.

10 From the *baccalauréat* to the *licence* and the *agrégation*, examiners are constrained to lower their demands on specific knowledge in order to maintain the level of linguistic standards: 'The essential thing is that it be well written.' Speaking of the examination for entry to the École normale, C. Bouglé wrote: 'It is formally understood that even for the essay in history, which presupposes knowledge of various bodies of fact, the examiners must give special attention to qualities of composition and exposition' (*Humanisme, sociologie, philosophie: Remarques sur la conception française de la culture générale*, Travaux de l'École normale supérieure (Hermann et Cie, Paris, 1938), p. 21). The reports of the *agrégation* and the C.A.P.E.S. are full of statements of this kind.

11 In the survey of student attitudes towards their studies based on a sample in which the marginal disciplines were less well represented, this inverse relationship between social origin and academic success (as measured by the number of honours grades) did not appear (cf. Bourdieu and Passeron, *Les Étudiants et leurs études*, p. 63); whereas in the present study, in which students who have a poorer rate of success constitute nearly half the sample, success appeared less directly linked to social origin. Similarly, Himmelweit and co-authors, comparing 40 'under-achieving' students with 40 'over-achieving' students at the London School of Economics, did not discover any significant differences according to socio-economic background or the cultural level of the parents (H. T. Himmelweit, T. Hilde and A. Summerfield, 'Student selection,

an experimental investigation', *British Journal of Sociology*, 3 (Dec. 1951)). The studies of Worswick and Evans on Oxford and Cambridge would seem to indicate in fact that in universities, inequalities in the rate of selection of students from different backgrounds are so strong that an inverse correlation between social class and results is observed (G. D. Worswick, 'The anatomy of Oxbridge', *Times Educational Supplement*, 3 May 1957; T. R. W. Evans 'The physiognomy of Cambridge', *Times Educational Supplement*, 16 Oct. 1959). Malleson observes the same inverse correlation between father's social class and results at University College, London (N. Malleson, 'University student, 1953 II. Schooling', *Universities Quarterly*, 14, no. 1, 1959, Jan. 1960, pp. 42–56).

12   Cf. Bourdieu and Passeron, *Les Étudiants et leurs études*, part 2.

13   In contrast to the working classes, for whom over-selection continues to be the rule, the category represented by the children of artisans and shopkeepers has greatly benefited from the expansion of the social basis of university recruitment (rising from 3.8% to 12.5% between 1939 and 1959), doubtless under the impact of a relative increase in the standard of living and in connection with the appearance within these groups of middle-class attitudes towards school. Now the children of artisans and shopkeepers are no less remote than working-class children from the verbal habits required by school; so it is not surprising that, being less rigorously selected, but from family settings as culturally unfavourable, they obtain the weakest results on all tests: only 40.5% of children from these backgrounds obtain a mark greater than 12 on the definitions test, as against 57% of upper-class children and 53% of working-class students. On the other hand, by comparison with male students from senior-management backgrounds, who have results superior to all other groups when they come from *lycées* and the weakest results when they come from *collèges*, the children of artisans and shopkeepers remain on the bottom rung, whether they have pursued their studies in a public or a private establishment. As to the children of middle-level managers, they obtain results which, although somewhat better, present an analogous structure, and which should be understood in terms of the same logic.

14   An earlier survey of medical students conducted by the Centre de sociologie Européenne showed that the average number of persons from the extended family who had completed or were engaged in higher education ranged from 1 in the case of lower-status children to 4 for those from senior-management backgrounds. This contrasts with the chances of access to higher education for individuals, which vary from 1 to 40 as between these two social groups. This gives a very good indication that students from the disadvantaged classes who do reach higher education came from families with a distinctive cultural milieu, at least in offering a much stronger subjective hope of going to university. Cf. P. Bourdieu and J.-C. Passeron, *Les Héritiers* (Ed. de Minuit, Paris, 1964), p. 44.

15   If we know, e.g., that as we ascend the commonly recognized hierarchy of educational institutions, the proportion of upper-class students regularly grows (until it reaches 51 per cent at the École normale supérieure and 57% at the École polytechnique, as against 28.5% for all French universities), we can

derive from the model of relationships between degree of selection and degree of success the working hypothesis that as over-selection of middle-class and working-class students is greatest in the *grandes écoles*, the correlation between results and social background will be completely reversed.

16 In general, the hierarchy of the different faculties on student test scores coincides in large measure with the hierarchy of faculties based on the proportion of students enjoying the greatest advantages of family background. The children of senior managers make up 52.2% of the sample in Paris, 49.3% at Lyon, 41.2% at Dijon, 24% at Lille and 13.6% at Rennes; on the other hand, the students who took Latin and Greek constitute 35.5% of the Paris sample, 26.7% of the sample at Lyon, 29.5% at Dijon, 24.3% at Rennes and 14.3% at Lille. Median results on the definitions test for students from these faculties were 13.7 for Paris, 13 for Lyon, 12.2 for Dijon, 10.7 for Lille and 10 for Rennes. Multivariate analysis shows that if we control for the action of social-advantage factors, the results of the Parisian students always remain superior to those of provincial students, and this holds across all subgroups. Indeed, in Paris, 79% of students who had the most classical training, 67% of those who received training on the modern side and 63% of those who took Latin only obtained more than 12 on the definitions test, as against 54%, 45.5% and 42.5% of students from the provinces. Male students as well as female students, philosophy students as well as sociology students, those from *lycées* as well as those from private schools, obtain better results in Paris than in the provinces.

17 Indeed, if, as Paul Clerc remarks, we see a certain democratization at work in the recruitment of students at the level of the *sixième*, working-class children still make for *collèges* more often than *lycées*; more than one-quarter leave these establishments in the two years which follow, and very few among them have the firm intention of persevering with their studies up to the *baccalauréat* (Paul Clerc, 'La famille et l'orientation scolaire au niveau de la sixième. Enquête de juin 1963 dans l'agglomération parisienne', *Population*, no. 4 (Aug.–Sept. 1964), p. 617). Receiving little or only poor support from their families, there is every chance that they will never reach higher education. If a proportion – necessarily the smallest – of the beneficiaries of this democratization of secondary education were to reach university despite everything, they would be burdened with the most unfavourable academic and cultural background (training on the modern side in a college, a family cultural background more unfavourable than that of students of the same social origin currently in higher education). There is every temptation that we might then come to speak of a 'decline in standards', forgetting the social implications of this phenomenon.

18 In a cohort of male students (all social classes combined), the chances of being in an arts faculty were 23 in 100; but among female students the chances were 52.8 in 100, more than double.

19 Cf. table 1.6.

20 In the control groups of *lycée* pupils, comprising 305 final-year students drawn from Paris and the provinces, girls obtain results equal to or even superior to boys: on the 'malapropism' test (scored negatively), the median was 9.5 for

boys and 9.1 for girls; on the language of humanism test, the results were respectively 5.5 and 5.4.

21   In 1962–3, according to B.U.S. statistics, girls represented 46.8% of students in the sub-final-year and 50.6% in final-year classes in public *lycées*.

22   We know that until 1925 young girls had to take supplementary courses in classical languages when they wished to obtain the *baccalauréat*, since the programmes designed in 1881 for the *lycées*, *collèges* and *cours secondaires* normally reserved the teaching of classical languages for boys' schools.

23   Coding favoured the emergence of a threshold since, by systematically abstaining from answering, a mark of 10 (5 × 2) could be obtained. For example, for a given word like 'cadastral', the coding instructions were very strict: Mark of 1: presence of themes bearing no relation to the semantic field of the word. Mark of 2: no response. Mark of 3: idea of document attesting property in land. Mark of 4: elaboration of all the particular features entering into the definition of 'cadastral' (a document which, on a community scale, defines property in land and serves as a basis for the allotment of land-tax), the enumeration not being formulated in a syntactic form aimed at reproducing the logical order of the definition. Mark of 5: syntactic arrangement of the definition (construction of the sentence according to the principle: identification of the proximate genus and precise formulation of specific differences in such a way that they pertain to the whole definition and to the definition only); and complete enumeration of the specific features of the cadastral.

Marks less than 10 were almost exclusively the domain of individuals who obtained a mark of 1 on several definitions – i.e., individuals who, being totally ignorant of the meaning of the word, proposed way out definitions. But it is precisely this group of 'bluffers' or the unthinking who are completely absent from the preparatory classes.

24   For the test on technical language, where it was the number of mistakes that was recorded, the divergence in results is also quite plain, the mode varying from 8 to 7 and the median from 8.3 to 6.9 as we pass from the preliminary-year university students to preparatory-class students; and the two distributions have on the whole a normal trend. For the preparatory-class students the same phenomenon was found as was observed in the case of the definitions test, though to a lesser extent – i.e., the absence of very weak individuals (having more than 11 mistakes).

25   This mainly concerns students who are preparing simultaneously for diplomas in several degree programmes: either *licence* in philosophy and *licence* in sociology, *licence* in sociology and *licence* in psychology, or *licence* in sociology and *licence* in literature. This group also includes students who seem to have attached themselves to no particular academic curriculum – i.e., the most dilettante element of the student population.

26   In fact a discipline as highly consecrated as philosophy can attract relatively heterogeneous students – and it is this very aspect which distinguishes it from sociology – doubtless because the prestige which it enjoys will draw not only the students best adapted to the academic world but also those least adapted to it. Thus, in the most academic tests, the philosophy group displays the highest

inter-quartile range; i.e., in this course the weakest students are particularly weak, and the strong are particularly strong.

27 Philosophy students are proportionately twice as likely as sociology students to be under 21 years (47.5%). The majority of the latter (57%) are aged 21–24 years, while students in mixed courses are divided equally between these ranges.

28 Nearly half the sociology students come from private establishments, as against only 27% for philosophy students, the largest proportion of whom (59%) come from *lycées*.

29 Philosophy students constitute the group which has most often received the most classical training (33.6%, as against 20.5% of students doing mixed courses and 30% of sociology students).

30 The traditional representation of the hierarchy of curriculum streams has hardly begun to lose its influence today. The pre-eminence of the classical streams used to be such that we could hardly speak of 'guidance', since curriculum stream was determined in quasi-automatic fashion by success measured on a scale of unique and unquestioned values, and since entry to the modern section was perceived by all, including the students themselves, as a relegation and downfall. We read in the preface to the instructions relative to the application of the 1925 plan for secondary education:

> This separation [of 'modern' pupils], as well as other factors which came to be associated with it, especially the low level of recruitment to stream B, did much to perpetuate the disfavour that was attached from the beginning to an education without Latin and to keep those pupils who did follow it in a humble situation. Such was the cause which is still very much alive today, the prejudice that the value of an education depends on the subjects which make it up, and that if classical education is pre-eminent, this is because it includes Latin and Greek in its programmes. (*Journal Officiel*, 3 Sept. 1925).

31 Another indication that knowledge of Latin and Greek does not produce a scholastic advantage in itself, independently of the pedagogical context in which it was acquired, is the fact that *lycée* students taking Greek and Latin – proportionately a smaller group than private school students (25.8%, as against 31.1%) – nevertheless obtained better results. Further, the group of students hailing from *lycées* who took neither Latin nor Greek obtained better results than those who took Latin and Greek but came from private establishments.

32 It is among young people who have done Latin and Greek that the number of students with a high success rate is proportionately greatest (36%), but also among whom the number of students with weak results is also proportionately greater (46.5%) than it is among students in the modern stream. (Cf. J.-C. Passeron and M. de Saint Martin, *Les Étudiants en médecine*, Cahier ronéotypé, Centre de sociologie Européenne, 1964.)

33 Moreover, the examination system is not the only thing in question. Even when verbal ease constitutes no explicit part of their rhetorical demands,

teachers whose whole training inclines them to take it for granted tend to reintroduce this requirement implicitly. In other words, the objective demands of an examination system cannot be dissociated from the use which teachers make of them, since it is they who monopolize the interpretation, the manipulation and the evaluation of them.

34   The proportion of students who obtained good academic results varies from 21% to 39% as we pass from students who have done neither Latin nor Greek to those who have received the most classical training.

35   The mechanism of this conversion is not reducible to the influence of material conditions. If, in a sample of students from the *sixième*, the proportion of 'good pupils' rises as a function of family income, Paul Clerc has been able to show that, at an equal level of qualifications, income (closely linked, as we know, to the educational level of the head of the family) exercises no additional influence on academic success, and that, on the contrary, at an equal level of income, the proportion of good students increases in a very significant fashion depending on whether the head of the family lacks a qualification or whether he holds the *baccalauréat*; this permits us to conclude that the influence of family background on academic success is, in the present situation, almost exclusively cultural. (Cf. Clerc, 'La famille et l'orientation scolaire'). In fact, we have to take into account not only the cultural level of the father and the mother, but also that of the ascendants of each branch of the family. Thus the influence of social origin on cultural practices and knowledge is more evident if we measure it not only at the level of the occupational category of the father, but include that of both the father and the grandfather. (Cf. Bourdieu and Passeron, *Les Étudiants et leurs études*, pp. 96–7.)

36   Cf. appendix 3.

37   Investigations in progress are seeking to determine what types of relationship to family values and what structures within the constellation of the family (e.g., cultural homogeneity or heterogeneity of the extended family) may lead a senior manager's child towards squandering, rather than fully utilizing, his cultural heritage and the working-class child towards academic keenness, rather than resignation.

38   At the probationary examination of 1964 [first part of the *baccalauréat* when this became internal – trans.] the success rate for public school candidates was 65%, as against 52% for candidates from private schools. Despite this first selection, the superiority of public school candidates remains evident at the *baccalauréat* itself (66%, as against 61%; cf. *Informations statistiques*, no. 66 (Jan. 1965)). If these differences may be attributed, at least in part, to the fact that private establishments recruit rejects, the private schools cannot have the same refuge function for working-class students, which explains why, whatever the establishment they attended during their secondary education, these students have a higher rate of success on the definitions test than those from privileged family backgrounds who did attend private establishments.

39   Thus we should keep in mind that working-class students have taken Latin three times less often than students from all socially advantaged backgrounds.

40   Whatever their training at secondary school, middle-class students consistently obtain the weakest results (in all cases more than half the individuals from this background receive less than 12); this tends to confirm the model put forward above (p. 42) to explain their poor results.

41   The aim of this questionnaire was to measure understanding of the language of teaching as actually used; and, difficult and unjustifiable as this language is in some of its terms, we have therefore not eliminated words where the probability of error approached certitude. But relieved of terms which appeared only once in the analysed literature and for which the frequency of error exceeded 80%, this questionnaire would be able to measure quite accurately – as the correlation between the results on the tests and on exams proves – the chances of students entering the cycle of the *licence* and pursuing without interruption studies in philosophy and the human sciences (at least in their present form). In reproducing the questionnaire, we have marked with an asterisk those items which it would be appropriate to suppress for such a purpose. [Note cued by * in original questionnaire – trans.]

2

Student Rhetoric in Exams

Christian Baudelot

This analysis of the rhetoric used by students in examinations is based on 160 papers in ethics and sociology and in general sociology submitted and corrected in Paris in the sessions of October 1962 and June 1963. The results need to be interpreted with care. With a limited and non-random sample of candidates, for whom background information such as occupational class was not available, there was no question of examining relationships between rhetorical form and student characteristics. Rather, the study aims to highlight some of the prevailing types of linguistic misunderstanding found in examination papers, to identify a collection of rhetorical traits rarely recognized as such, but which play an important role in marking, and to outline a number of hypotheses concerning these.[1]

* * *

The essay is the sole means of expression officially reserved to the student to respond to the professorial lecture. It is also the only evidence open to the professor to assess the student. The seriousness of this enterprise, at once a rejoinder, a plea and an exhibit in proof, escapes none of the protagonists. Yet all agree in refusing to take seriously the sole technical means of satisfying the requirements of these multiple roles – rhetoric. With its gratuitous formalism, the essay would seem to detract from the prestigious image of themselves which academics and students both like to project. Rather than take the essay for what it is – an imposed test in rhetoric – they prefer to take it for what it is not – a free and personal creation. Unanimously endured as a fate for which teacher, no more than student, can feel responsible, it is remarkable that an essay topic is never seen as being imposed, but is rather 'offered' for the 'attention' of the candidate, who is 'invited to compose'. Famous prescriptions for composing essays, far from supplying the basic principles of logic and rhetoric, usually try to persuade the student that this 'literary genre' is first and foremost a matter of taste, and requires from those who would practise it a set of gifts which cannot be methodically acquired.

> In the essay as in every literary genre the right *tone* must be found; to depart from it is to create a true artistic dissonance. . . . This *tone* is much more a matter of culture and of personal gifts than theory; it should be neither vulgar nor familiar. . . . But how impossible it is to lay down general prescriptions on the art of making a plan! As hard, indeed, as to teach the art of thinking! Each of us can only learn [the art of essay writing] alone, with plenty of books, plenty of time, and a great deal of 'spirit', as the eighteenth century tells us.[2]

Ritually placed under the aegis of Pascal, Boileau or Voltaire, the 'general directions on the art of writing' – when eventually delivered – turn out to be mere precepts and golden rules. The technical means which might allow them to be applied are never made explicit.

> In an essay on aesthetics, good style must be most completely integrated with composition; it is this element which fuels the impulse of each paragraph by creating an ever more forceful impression of analysis. Golden rule of the plan: don't be a mere division into sections, translate the deeper movement of mind . . . in short, be the very emanation of spirit. . . . A conclusion gains in brilliance, a little filled out; like the introduction, it is thus a purple passage. . . . Students should aim to succeed in writing, firstly through care and clarity (which will be sufficient); then (for some) through vigour and personality.[3]

Resigned to convention or routine, when teachers choose from a narrow range of largely general topics, they are confirming the fact that the essay genre is really only a pretext for them, and that they are ready to pay homage to the creative liberty of the student who will measure the 'beauty' of a topic by the extent of its generality. 'Thanks to the fullness of perspective which it opened up, this topic was one of those which allow candidates to reveal not only their capacity for personal reflection, but the quality of their culture and the reach of their knowledge.'[4]

The level of generality of essay topics is amply illustrated by the fact that 25 of the 30 topics set for the sociology exams by the Faculty of Arts in

Paris between June 1945 and October 1961 contained the terms 'sociology', 'society' or 'social'. Sixteen of the 30 were on the scope and nature of the discipline – sociology and psychology, sociology and history (three times), sociology and ethnology, sociology and geography, sociology and economics – or on social morphology or methodology – laws in sociology (three times), typology of global societies, the notion of structure, the distinction between normal and pathological (twice). The remaining 14 topics called for reflection on social facts – social division of labour (three times), constitutive elements of a society, technology, works of civilization and culture, restricted or particular groups.

The list of these 30 topics, some of which rotate in a cycle, is the exact reflection of the official programme, and their fidelity to the certificate in sociology goes so far as to systematically ban every topic that is not general. Monotony and fidelity to the course are even greater in the sociology paper for the certificate in ethics and sociology: 13 of the 21 topics dealt with problems posed by the relationship between ethics and sociology, between the social and the moral, the individual and society.

The way instructions are actually worded in exam questions comes down to three traditional types. From a selection of 111 topics, 45 were presented as general themes for reflection: for example, examine the concept of authority; consider law from a sociological point of view; review the notion of a free act. Associating or opposing two concepts was the approach adopted in 38 topics: for example, sociology and psychoanalysis, causality and finality; while 25 questions invited the candidate to 'comment and discuss' judgements of set authors. There were three topics in general philosophy which did not conform to these three types:

'Is philosophy in your view a project of mediation or an attempt to comprehend immediate givens, or are there other possible roles for philosophy?' (Paris, June 1955)

'Philosophers have often posed the problem of the reality of the external world. How would you formulate this problem? What solution would you offer?' (Paris, October 1958)

'Can we view the reality of the external world as a problem? Has it been solved, and, if not, how would you attempt to solve it?' (Paris, June 1958)

Refuse to pose precise questions; solicit personal views on final solutions to problems without solutions and perspectives on topics which are open-ended; invite the candidate to engage in anti-rhetoric; and glorify the whole exercise with the vocabulary of intellectual creation – the setting of the essay topic is an attempt to escape the unreal character of the essay by a complete lack of realism, and to transform what is essentially a scholastic test in rhetoric into a project of inspired creativity. Deny them, refuse them, scorn them, ignore them – rhetorical skills are still among the fundamental criteria of academic judgement.

That particular 'know-how' which the teacher neither teaches nor openly demands, he still looks for 'in expression and in discussion and in composition', but fails to find:

> An essay can be just average because there is too little evidence of reflection or knowledge, but still show an element of technical mastery; now in fact it is this quality of technical competence which all candidates most lacked. . . . The best papers also picked up marks for style; firm and clear presentations gained over loose, rough and careless efforts in which a scattering of simple notions were piled up without any great discernment. . . . Clumsiness of expression was the rule; few essays displayed any elegance. The art of the well-chosen phrase is declining; we found it only here and there.[5]

Comments written at the top of examination scripts testify to the prodigious attention which examiners give to formal qualities: the *art of composition* – 'well constructed', 'badly organized', 'well handled', 'coherent paper', 'nicely arranged discussion', 'no plan', 'unable to plan', 'disorder' – then *style* – 'poorly expressed', 'unclearly written', 'disgraceful', 'loose', 'distorted', 'rough', 'good qualities of expression', 'firm presentation', 'balanced', 'precise', 'elegant', 'fluent', 'felicitous wording'. Margins are often littered with the peremptory 'badly put'.

These evaluations never contain any remarks which go to the substance of the discussion, and their resolutely *judicatory* tone belies those declarations which represent the essay as the occasion of a genuine exchange between creator and connoisseur. Before dividing a paper into its qualities and its faults, the examiner delivers a global judgement, without appeal, which is merely the verbal translation of the numerical mark – 'good', 'very good', 'good paper', 'serious work', 'bad', 'very uneven', 'off the point', 'inadequate', 'inept', 'weak', 'excellent', 'superior', 'nil'. Professorial judgement is passed in the name of criteria which have never been made explicit and which demand from the candidate conformity to an intellectual role more than a demonstration of specific skills. 'The best papers in the history of philosophy examination were impressive because their authors remained philosophers throughout. Their success was due above all to the fact that particular historical references were subordinated to conceptions of the progress of scientific reason which had a richness and true philosophical character.'[6]

Finally, professorial judgement is not loath to resort openly to the pretext of the text to judge the author in his very essence – 'qualities of thought', 'qualities of mind', 'qualities of shrewdness', 'original mind',

'Your ideas lack consistency', 'You have a philosophical head'. As an inspector-general declares:

> Only a mind that is well-nourished and trained, a thinker who can turn the chief areas of his knowledge into a culture, can work with real result. Only too easily, therefore, essays expose the indigent, the disarmed, the awkward, the puny; . . . into the clear light of day they draw the varied faults of mind. What excellent revealers of quality they really are! Well can we understand why teachers stick with them and students dread them.[7]

School is able to make the manipulation of the language of ideas the unquestionable sign of human and personal qualities, and the essay can be this dramatic enterprise of gambling a future on words; but all the while teachers and students never cease to share their contempt for the art of rhetoric. Their scorn may be simply a mask against self-contempt; perhaps by concealing the true criteria of academic judgement from themselves, along with the particular cultural qualities which these sanction, they may succeed in forgetting just what the concepts of 'eloquence', 'ease' and 'richness' (even philosophical) owe to the ethos of a class.

* * *

Research into the factors which have the strongest influence on academic marking shows that it is inequalities in linguistic performance which most strongly differentiate good from bad scripts. It is significant that marks tend to fall as more and more of the traits are found which, according to Bernstein, distinguish working-class from upper-class speech patterns.[8] As these features recede, on the other hand, marks rise, responding to the qualities of complex and differentiated language peculiar to the cultivated classes.[9] It is to these qualities that we now turn.

Degree of syntactic complexity

A high proportion of essays which receive poor marks use short sentences; these sentences are grammatically simple and syntactically poor, with independent or main clauses governing one or two subordinate, mainly relative clauses. The type of sentence found in the best scripts, on the other hand, is full of epithets and appositions, qualifications and refinements, and multiplies complexities of every kind.

> The truth is − and as the hyper-empirical dialectic itself demands (and we have every reason to submit to its requirements, which are legitimate

provisionally and from the methodological point of view) – this test would only really be such were it extended to the infinite repertory of global societies and to other deeper strata that have existed at some point in time or are still in existence, which, obviously enough, could not be attempted here. (mark: 13/20)

Or:

Through this, the religious colouration having progressively disappeared to make way only for the irrational pursuit of profit conceived as an end in itself, without even the correlative appearance of a hedonist or eudemonist orientation, capitalism has been able to become the representative type of a purely finalist and utilitarian ethics, that is, an immoral pragmatism. (mark: 12.5/20)

It is striking that the concessive conjunctions (though, although) are continually employed only in scripts marked above 12. The great majority of papers which scored between 0 and 12 contained none, but every paper above that mark contained at least two, some as many as four. Similarly, the frequency of comparatives is proportional to the mark: in the better scripts they occur more often, in the weaker scripts they are rarer.

Use of conjunctions

Average and poor scripts also stand out from better papers by the use of a limited number of conjunctions, often employed in the wrong way: 'thus', 'so', 'also', 'consequently', 'but', 'indeed', 'for', 'rather', 'more', 'besides', 'then'.

After a general and irrelevant development of the topic, a candidate primes the conclusion: '*So*, now we can *thus* give a clear and precise definition of social obligation as sketched out above. It is moral obligation towards society. That is what makes it social.' The particles 'so' and 'thus' do not correspond to any real connection between ideas; they are there simply to introduce the conclusion. Similarly, there is a break between the tautology of fact (which appears in the definition) and the proclamation of an impending 'clear and precise definition' which is supposed to follow from the preceding 'sketch'. This testifies to the mimetic posture of the student, whereby he retains from professorial language only the external signs of coherence.

By contrast, marks go up as the range of particles and conjunctions expands – 'nevertheless', 'still', 'although', 'however', 'doubtless', 'certainly', 'assuredly', 'from then', 'correlatively'. Most of these conjunctions, by comparison with the group found in poorer scripts, imply a more complex syntactic construction, and more directly involve the meaning of the phrases they introduce. It is not by chance, as we shall see, that this meaning tends to be restrictive.

Use of adjectives and adverbs

In weaker papers, a limited number of adverbs and adjectives recur at regular intervals, and serve to stress particular observations, rather than actually modifying the meaning of the nouns and verbs that they accompany: 'fundamentally', 'essentially', 'precisely', 'absolutely', 'exactly', 'uniquely', 'only', 'fundamental', 'essential', 'absolute', 'precise'. For example, 'The notion of moral purity could only have a meaning *precisely* in the world of history in which man endlessly transforms himself.'

Wealth of vocabulary

Metaphors and technical terms occur only above a certain level of performance. None of the following words appears in scripts marked below 12: 'reification' appears (five times in those marked above 12), 'adequation' (six times), 'insertion' (five times), 'coincidence' (nine times), 'specificity' (four times), 'asymptotic' (twice), 'colinearity' (twice), 'hedonist' and 'eudemonist' (once), 'dissolve' (four times), 'invest', 'disinvest', 'reinvest' (three times).

Selection of groups of sequences

Frequent use of completely idiomatic expressions which operate as syntactic 'habits' is one of those traits which average or poor exam papers share with 'public language'. Professorial language has a predilection for tropes which concede complexity while preserving unity – 'If it is true that . . . it is no less true that' – or which maintain the coexistence of apparent contraries – 'While . . . however . . .'. Others are employed to differentiate meaning by drawing contrasts: 'It is not so much that . . . as . . .'; 'We can say, not that . . . but we cannot say that . . .'; 'Not . . . but . . .'; 'Far from . . . on the contrary . . .'; 'It is not a matter of . . . but . . .'. Still others aim at demolishing commonly held preconceptions: 'Contrary to what we often think', 'In spite of the commonly held view', 'Today we no longer ask ourselves whether . . .'. Borrowed from professorial language, these tropes are employed in a mechanical fashion in poorer examination scripts, where they are transposed from the domain of nuance to that of macroscopic assertion.

'If Thrasymachus is right, Rousseau is not wrong.' 'It is thus necessary to accept this mystification, but one cannot but criticize it.' 'Purity is less a mirage than an objective reality . . .'. 'We can say that the moral life does not coincide with social life, but we cannot say the moral life is without connection with social life.' 'If man is a free being, he is also exposed to a nature rebellious and dialectically opposed to spirit, namely the body.' 'If reality prevents us from affirming that things second are not the cause of things first, we must admit that a society will only be sound when the two systems are able to co-exist smoothly.' 'Contrary to what we often think, ethics is not only concerned with the individual.'

Less and less decontextualized as the mark rises, these tropes are present at all levels of performance, but end up supplying the best scripts with some fine distinctions. 'It would appear that Eros is the best example: not that of Agathon, beautiful god, pure, but that of Diotima, poorly attired, dirty hands.' (mark: 14/20).

The limitations of our empirical data − like the limited state of recruitment to higher education itself − do not allow us to deduce from the existence of traits common to the speech of working-class families and the poorer examples of student discourse that the authors of these poor scripts are indeed drawn disproportionately from working-class families. But such a comparison does have the merit of showing that professorial judgement, by privileging a complex and differentiated language and by devaluing uniformity of expression, tends to reappropriate the cultural values of the elite. At the same time, academic discourse, through its hierarchy of formal criteria, favours students from bourgeois backgrounds, who rediscover in its medium their natural linguistic milieu, and sets further obstacles in the path of working-class students.

* * *

Essay-writing rhetoric at its lowest level turns to magic to exorcize error. Equipped with an apparatus of words whose meanings are understood less than the rhetorical power that can be mobilized through them, students pull in terms and expressions blindly derived from professorial discourse as if merely invoking them will liberate the mana contained therein and render them efficacious.

Words like 'structure', 'structural', 'dialectic', 'ontological', 'essence', 'determinism', 'alternative', 'rational', 'rationality', 'system', 'systematic', and 'function' are employed more for their philosophical sonority than *stricto sensu*. Iterative formulations are developed from the same group of sounds: 'There is an ambiguity infinitely ambiguous'; 'The consciousness of univocity is equivocal'; 'The least impurity at the heart of purity is there still impurity;

contrariwise, purity at the heart of impurity does not mean purity, but rather impurity . . .'. This magical enterprise can rise to the level of hermetics: 'Purity is this oblique, indirect regard which causes the idea of purity as of the abstract presence of the omni-absent omni-presence to spring dialectically forth from the heart of conscience.' Or it can resort at grand ceremonial moments to ready-made, universally applicable sequences, as in this conclusion: 'A dialectical transcendence of this alternative is possible, perhaps; however, taking such a road risks giving the individual who sets out on it a feeling of reassurance, rather than resolving affectively and rationally at one and the same time the basic question which still remains posed.'

While this rite of exorcism over-values the power of words, a more prophylactic technique involves conjuring up spells by the multiplication of gestures of prudence. Working at a level of verbal manipulation which is not so blind, deliberate attention is given to diverting the examiner by depriving him of every opportunity of detecting true error in the web of rhetorical language. The student ensures that each affirmation is qualified by the possibility of its negation, and situates the discussion at such a great distance from concrete example that while he, for his part, would find it difficult to prove the necessity of any proposition, it becomes impossible for the examiner to prove that anything is false. These techniques include:

(a) *The use of indefinite expressions*: 'It is said'; 'Some people believe'; one, some, something ('*One type of* society is defined by *an* equilibrium between *certain* social phenomena'); something ('To be thinking *the idea of something* already implies *some* possibility of realizing that thing').

(b) *Attenuations*, which imply that the contrary proposition is not impossible, and transfer to the examiner the task of excluding any consideration which would actually introduce doubt – 'sufficiently', 'in general', 'often', 'sometimes', 'in a way', 'in certain respects', 'in one sense'. 'Nearly all philosophers have thought that . . .'. 'Ethics is, in a way, only constituted as ethics in order to palliate that impurity which we can almost say is essential to man.'

(c) *Timid approximations*: perhaps, a kind of tension, a type of contradiction.

(d) *False particularization*: 'a specific society', 'a particular moral attitude', 'in a given situation', 'such and such'.

(e) *False exemplification*: 'Let us take the example of Promethean societies: the moral response to a given situation will be different according to the type of society because each society's vision of the world is different.' 'It is thus, for example, that the various forms of personal moral life also depend on social factors . . .'. Or, better still, 'So according to the type of society, be it industrial or archaic, and within industrial societies themselves, there exist moral attitudes particular to each society, for within each society, cultures, attitudes differ, and also moral conduct; according to the society and its cultural works, there is a particular moral attitude.'

(f) *Absence of examples*.

(g) *'Purple' truths*: 'There are several kinds of societies.'

(h) *Empty abstraction*: 'There is scarcely a concept found in ethics which, one day or other, could not be turned against the essence of the ethical demand, always present and never defined.' A fine example of the not-even-false, this sentence contains four examples of abstract generality ('moral', 'essence', 'concept', 'ethical demand'), an attenuation (negative construction) which is reinforced by the 'scarcely', and the uncertainty of the 'one day or other'. Its concluding phrase is masterly, for it provides a justification of the not-even-false by dispensing the candidate from defining what is not defined.

(i) *Peremptory tone* of the doctoral presentation, stripped of everything problematic, or juxtaposition of various views appearing over time: 'Compte says . . . ; later Marx will say . . . ; and Mauss . . . ; and Weber. . . .'

(j) *Prophylactic relativism*, the doctrinal basis underlying two-thirds of the scripts in the sample: 'A static definition of human reality cannot be given; a formula is thus never wholly true or wholly false. However, to the extent that it shocks, it set us thinking.'

Born of an obsession with avoiding error at all costs, this intellectual timidity stands in marked contrast to the rhetorical ease of those candidates whose deployment of the irrefutable signs of personal culture protects their scripts from the possibility of error, while bringing their reflections no closer to truth or reality.

Remarkably, all scripts marked over 12 quoted Plato, Seneca or Weber in the original, while only 6 per cent of other papers followed this procedure. Similarly, while two-thirds of all papers marked between 8 and 12 mentioned the names and works of more than five authors (some relying on 10 or 12), 70 per cent of scripts marked above 12 cited only two or three authors whose views were analysed at greater length, often establishing quotations in their correct context. Some candidates took this care for accuracy to the point of erudite display:

The case of Hegel is singular: in studying the writings of his youth, we can see how his thought progressed from a study of Kantian ethics applied to Scripture – *The Life of Jesus*, written in 1794 – to critical reflections on the tragic character of religion – *The Positivity of Christianity* (1796), *The Spirit of Christianity and its Destiny* (1797) – and, thanks to a reading of James Stewart between 1798 and 1800, then (at the same time as he composed at Jena between 1801 and 1807 the lectures which Hoffmeister has gathered together under the title of *Realphilosophie*) through a reflection on the treatise of the

Wealth of Nations by Adam Smith, to the *Phenomenologie des Geistes* (1807), which is, as recent works have shown, as much a social pedagogy as a pedagogy of consciousness, and on to the later writings, of which only traces are conserved. (mark: 13/20)

Or again:

(Cf. *Critique de la raison dialectique*, vol. 1, pages 301–3 at the note.) Similarly when we take account of the genesis of the ethical, as praxis in relation to the Other, shedding its own light on the basis of material conditions (Sartre describes the first moment of this, that of the radical constitution of Evil, o[p]. c[it]., page 208) and of later peripeteia in the same fashion (cf. o[p]. c[it]., page 189, where the evolution of the problem of violence is resumed in the course of the development described there) . . .

Others practise the knowing allusion. Without explicitly invoking Plato or referring to the *Symposium*, the author of this script (already cited) writes: 'It would appear that Eros is the best example: not that of Agathon, beautiful god, pure, but that of Diotima, poorly attired, dirty hands: he is the "demon", that is, the mediator more than the intermediary' (mark: 14/20). And again: 'Heroes fail to attain this ideal: didn't the dream of Alcestis, just like that of Monime, establish this purity in human relationships? But Monime dies and Alcestis has to die in this world' (mark: 13.5/20).

The obviousness of a student's success in establishing a relationship with the unreal world of linguistic exchanges demanded by the academic game is very unequal, as high or low marks indicate. By preferring students who affect to prove that this unreality is in fact a real experience and who use rhetorical artifice to have the unreality of the rhetorical universe forgotten, the professor tries to conceal from himself the real character of an exercise which he feels bound to impose.

In average-quality scripts, there is a predominance of abstract modes of construction. Concrete modes of expression are qualified by restrictive phrasing ('in general', 'often', 'sometimes') or by neutral constructions (e.g., the use of the infinitive), and are tainted with a sense of the approximate through the recurring use of auxiliaries which promote artificiality ('should', 'must', 'can') and which lend themselves to hypothetical construction ('We must thus ask . . .'; 'It can also be said . . .').

In 72 per cent of essays, candidates begin their discussion under the shelter of myths or the ideas of various authorities;[10] but 70 per cent of the scripts which received the highest marks used the exordium to declare the student's personal interest in the task.

Significantly, and in contrast to the majority of other scripts, 90 per cent of those which scored over 12 frequently used the first-person singular, put actualizing phrases at the head of sentences ('In truth', 'As a matter of fact', 'In fact'), and preferred demonstrative to indefinite pronouns – '*This* anteriority proclaimed of an original purity'; 'We could thus define moral purity by *this* absolute coincidence between what I am and what I do'; 'It is *this* obedience to duty which establishes the ground of a good will'; 'It is *here* a matter of knowing whether yes or no'. They made extensive use of the reflexive pronoun 'itself', which was placed at the end of a sentence and acted as a clausula – 'Purity is not only the death of action, it is death itself, a logic irreducible to man himself.' But it is worth noting that this apparent personalization is itself also fictive. In an essay on purity, the 'personal and original' examples compared purity with water, fire, snow and crystal.

Always careful to deny the fictive nature of the exercise, 70 per cent of the best scripts stressed the difficulty and complexity of the topic at the outset or the exceptional interest which it held. 'To the extent that the pursuit of authenticity is central to *our* human thought, reason has every interest in this question' (mark: 12.5/20). 'The relationship between types of societies and moral attitudes is at once fundamental for understanding the existence of different types of societies, and their evolution, and the moral attitudes, consequences and causes of these evolutions' (mark: 13/20). 'To live humanly and to live morally, this is perhaps at bottom the sole, the unique problem given to man to resolve' (mark: 12.5/20).

The good paper also excels in deploying a truly dissertatory dramaturgy, flourishing interrogative and exclamatory turns of phrase: 'But this man, who is neither angel nor beast, is he then an intermediate being, half-angel, half-beast, a hybrid being? Certainly not!' (mark: 13/20). 'But who knows the chemical formula for moral purity?' (mark: 12.5/20). 'The instinct of good and evil, is it therefore acquired?' (mark: 12.5/20). 'For in the final analysis, what is purity?' (mark: 13/20).

Equally frequent are the imperatives 'Let us examine!', 'Let us study!', 'Let us conclude!' and metaphors derived from the register of physical violence: 'the idealist scandal', 'the confrontation of two antinomies', 'the desperate effort of a dialectic'. 'Ethics must clash with violence in order to achieve rigour. It is necessary to attain to the indignation, the revolt, the insolence of a Thrasymachus.' 'Spinoza put this question to us violently.'

* * *

By devaluing all the traits which make the essay only an essay and by rewarding a set of superficially anti-scholastic attitudes and postures, academics attach great importance to the student himself perpetuating the aristocratic fiction which makes the 'scholastic' attitude an execrable virtue in a scholastic world. Indeed, they demonstrate their indebtedness to students who perpetuate misunderstanding by recognizing them as worthy to perpetuate it. However, a finer analysis reveals that if good scripts display a different relationship to academic culture, they are as dependent as bad ones on the tropes of professorial language. Borrowings from the vocabulary of violence and action can thus, for example, peacefully coexist with the tropes of nuance, reticence and concession. Rather than choosing between the scholastic and the anti-scholastic, academics in fact select from a series of equally academic self-images which are reflected back to them in the language of their students. It is scarcely surprising if, under the circumstances, they prefer images which hold the advantage of reassuring them of their effectiveness as teachers, and that they refuse to recognize themselves in images which, if more realistic, threaten their good conscience and their personal comfort. If there is one image which is intolerable, it is the one which degrades them by simplifying their discourse. In his lecture the professor can declare, 'Purity is a mirage, but at the same time it is not a mirage.' However, he will never own up to being the instigator of this same thought when it figures prominently in a student essay or when it concludes an essay thus: 'If purity has a deceptive appearance, yet it is conceivable, and therefore possible.' Often observed in this study of student rhetoric, the clumsy or irrelevant reinstatement of tropes or words borrowed from professorial language – to which the professor magically opposes the disclaimer, 'But I never said that!' – is even more likely to be penalized when the professor, seeing his work in them, is forced to admit his own simplemindedness or, even worse, his inability to make himself understood. Equally, the professor little appreciates the too servile attitude which reminds him of the dependence which ties the candidate to the examiner. Appearing in mediocre or poor scripts, the dithyrambic elegies to the work of a master, the enthusiastic citation of his books or his lectures, the act of allying his name to the great thinkers of antiquity or of furiously espousing his quarrels – all are seen by him to whom they are addressed as betraying a narrow notion of the professorial mind which, on the contrary, proudly declares its limitless liberalism on the eve of the exams: 'Don't hesitate to put forward your own views!'; 'You don't have to adopt my views!'; 'Don't think you have to repeat everything I've told you!'. To a too close dependence on the academic world, the professor prefers the apparent offhandedness of those essay-writers who are sufficiently self-assured to deal as equals with their examiner. Responding to allusion with allusion, to nuance with nuance, to a language *ad usum delphini* with a discourse *ad usum magistri*, it is these students who confirm academics in the illusion that their teaching is not illusory.

*   *   *

Is it enough to demonstrate in the misinterpretations and the forgeries of student rhetoric the irrefutable proof that professorial language is not understood by its audience? Are we done with the essay once we conclude that a script receives a much better mark if it further perpetuates the miscomprehension which turns school into a place for the reciprocal and complicit exchange of innate qualities rather than for laborious apprenticeship? Not really. For the essay, as it is prepared and assessed under the current examinations regime, makes elegance, ease, assurance and distinction the true dissertatory qualities, and penalizes vulgarity of style, clumsiness of expression and awkwardness of formulation. Through dissertatory rhetoric, the ability to manipulate a language which remains the language of a social class, even when decorated with the values of universality, becomes the unique criterion of academic judgement, and the essay one of the most apt instruments for perpetuating cultural privilege.

NOTES

1 Research in progress aims to relate the character of examination scripts, success in oral and in written exams, and even the candidate's attitude towards the examiner to various social and scholastic attributes (from social origin to assiduousness during the year). As the research involves a faculty in which the traditional use of essays in examinations has been replaced by a series of questions which call for only brief expositions, we should be able to determine those categories of students who are advantaged by the different forms of the examination.

2 A. Chassang and C. Senninger, *La Dissertation littéraire générale* (Paris, Hachette, 1955) ch. 1: Conseils généraux.

3 Ibid.

4 *Rapport du jury d'agrégation de philosophie* (Paris, 1963).

5 Extracts from ibid.

6 Ibid.

7 R. Pons, Preface to Chassang and Senninger, *La Dissertation littéraire générale*.

8 B. Bernstein, 'Social class and linguistic development'. Based on empirical data, Bernstein's studies show that different forms of language use are developed differently among the different social classes. The middle classes cultivate within the speaking subject a theoretical attitude towards the structural possi-

bilities of syntactic organization, and turn speech into an autonomous activity, setting up a permanent invitation to qualified formulation. To this ultra-differentiated 'formal language' is opposed the 'public language' of the working classes. Syntactic rigidity and restricted use of the possibilities of language among these groups discourage the speaking subject from the verbal elaboration of subjective intentions, and little by little orient him towards descriptive rather than analytical concepts.

9   Marked in theory from 0 to 20, the essays in the sample were in fact marked from 6 to 14. Marks below 8 are uncommon (18%), while marks over 12 are still rarer (10%). Two-thirds of the scripts (67%) are grouped in half-points between 8 and 12.

10 In their first sentence, 72% of scripts invoke either an *author* – 'According to Durkheim'; 'Pascal said'; 'I see the good and I value it, but I do not do it'; 'Spinoza who cites Ovid, here rejoins St Paul' – or an *origin* – 'From the highest antiquity'; 'Already the moralists of antiquity' – or a *cardinal truth* – 'Man is in the first place a moral being'; 'Philosophy is doubt', 'All human action is ambiguous' – or *common sense* – 'It is often said'; 'It is commonly accepted that . . .'. From the moment it is adopted, this practice tends to detach the topic and the remarks that follow from any personal connection, by relegating them to the domain of myth, which amounts to proclaiming their unreality.

3

University Students and their Attitudes to Academic Staff and Teaching Practice

Guy Vincent
with the assistance of Michel Freyssenet

Introduction

In an era when ideologies of education put the teaching relationship in higher education on a level with economic and political conflict and see the demise of an 'education in culture' in the queue of new social strata at the door of the 'mass' university, sociological analysis needs to situate the teaching relationship and the attitudes of different groups of students firmly in the context of the social functions performed by academic institutions.

Within the scope of a pilot study, the whole range of issues bearing on the teaching relationship in higher education could not be dealt with adequately. Instead, the aim has been to develop suitable methods of approach and to form a necessarily broad view of the opinions and attitudes of university students.

Conducted in the 1963–4 academic year as part of the research programme of the sociology of education group in the Centre de Sociologie Européenne, the survey employed a questionnaire which was administered to lecture audiences of students in philosophy, sociology, and psychology, as well as to a number of control groups drawn from other disciplines.[1]

The questionnaire essentially addressed three points:[2] the image which students formed of higher education, based on their studies and on the goals they associated with it; their opinions about various forms of teaching (professorial lectures, practical classes, etc.); and their views about instructional technologies (board, textbook, television, etc.).[3]

From a sociological point of view, the teaching relationship brings together agent and user in an academic system which objectively performs a range of social functions. These functions or institutional ends coincide more or less with the goals pursued by the different social users of higher education. Male and female students, students from different social classes, at least dimly see the place and the destiny created for them in the wider society and also in the academic system which serves it. That is why it is important to try to capture differences in their perceptions of teaching and in their image of higher education.

Teaching methods and the teaching relationship which takes shape on the basis of these methods both depend on the nature of the institutional ends towards which, objectively, the academic system works.[4] When these functions undergo change and, more precisely, when the hierarchy of functions is thrown into confusion, or when the social users of the academic system seek to impose their own goals on its operation, the methods of teaching, from then on called 'traditional', come into question, and practices which were hitherto successful appear ineffective and ill-adapted. The users of the system put into play the social and cultural resources available to them, and in particular the largely inherited qualities which they derive from their social milieu. These cultural resources are more or less highly valued, depending on the operational criteria of the academic system, but, like the particular objectives being pursued by the different social users, they condition attitudes towards different teaching activities and towards different forms of teaching. That is why the focus of our student questionnaire was on various types of teaching presentation, the use of multicopied teaching materials, the role of small group discussions and so forth.

Using a questionnaire as the main source of information is, of course, not without its drawbacks. Questions which are too direct risk stereotyped answers. Deeper values and attitudes can always be confused with mere artefacts of the survey, and tendentious responses cannot be ruled out. The survey instrument covered issues on which students were very likely to have formed definite opinions because of widespread debate in public forums, the press and so on. Administered in March 1964, the survey followed hard on the heels of the university working groups and the debates surrounding their activity, so that students were already sensitized to teaching issues. In framing the questions, care was taken to avoid any allusion to these debates, and to avoid registering superficial and emotional responses to overt ideological positions.

In designing the questionnaire, we were able to draw on the results of previous research using open-ended questions and, in particular, on a series of group discussions and semi-structured interviews on teaching and on culture. Analysis of the content of these exchanges helped us achieve a fuller understanding of the meaning of responses to our questionnaire.

Finally, we have tried to measure attitudes to teaching in the most indirect way possible, sticking closely to the everyday language in which students themselves discuss educational issues. (More detailed remarks on the survey methodology are included in the appendix, following the questionnaire.)

The present report does not address all the survey results, but only those findings which fall into a fairly systematic pattern. Our conclusions draw on previous research, as well as the qualitative data from the pre-survey interviews and from the open-ended questions contained in the questionnaire itself.[5]

I   STUDENTS AND THE UNIVERSITY SYSTEM

Students were asked to identify the most characteristic feature of higher education as it is today, and then to say what ought to be the essential aims of the system. This line of enquiry was not intended as a kind of referendum, calling for fully deliberated and lucid responses. Rather, we were concerned with the range of student reactions to more or less stereotyped images of higher education, images which not only circulate in the public debates that are particularly frequent today, but which are formed through the way students are counselled by their teachers, through their day-to-day experience of how the system works, and through the results which the system actually delivers. Who the student is, his vision of the future, and the place he occupies in the system mean that we must expect a diversity of individual reactions which a few, rather caricatured cases will illustrate: the young woman whose studies 'might always turn out to be useful'; the male student, not much of a thinker, whose credential will represent social promotion; or the young man, sure of his future, who comes from another faculty to take a few arts exams as ornaments and proof of his personal superiority.

The population of the universities is changing, both in quality and in quantity, and the academic system, reacting to this challenge, endeavours to reaffirm its fundamental commitments. But to what extent do the different categories of today's students actually share these values?

Higher education and its ends

Appointed by tradition with the advancement and transmission of learning in its highest forms and as dispenser of the qualifications governing access to the learned professions, higher education represents itself, and outwardly appears in all its modalities of operation and in the demands which it makes, not as a system of vocational training, but as an education in culture. The reflections of the sage, the sane judgement and rational action of the honest man, the 'general culture' which confers those qualities of heart and mind unknown to the mere specialist, the humanist training which transcends the narrow limits of technical skill – these are so many manifestations of the ideal functioning of the academic system in its traditional form.

Our survey shows that even while outwardly contesting the system, university students remain at heart profoundly attached to its fundamental values.

A different result might well have been expected given the fact that the questionnaire, by providing a set list of real and ideal features, effectively invited students to search for contrasts between higher education as it currently operates and their ideal views of how it should operate. Taking one current stereotype as an example, the too theoretical and remote character of higher education, often denounced today, contrasts with the ideal of ethical training or with the ideology of 'commitment'. But, when graphically depicted (see appendix 1), the bars representing relative frequencies of real and ideal images indicate significant departures from the expected pattern. Even though the design of the questionnaire tended to favour explicit contrasts,[6] the real image chosen is not simply the reverse of an ideal image.[7]

This suggests that a significant section of the student population shares the institutional values of the system (such as these are perceived), or approves of certain essential features of it as coinciding with their own ideals. Their affirmativeness is greatest when it comes to three of the aims which are most traditionally and most frequently proclaimed to be essential to the work of higher education: cultivation of a critical spirit, transmission of general culture and promotion of research.[8] For example, it might be thought that students who see the transmission of 'general culture' as the most distinctive feature of higher education as it operates today would tend to be those whose ideal would place much greater stress on the transmission of specialized knowledge and skills or the provision of vocational training. But, on the contrary, the selection of 'general culture' to describe the contemporary functioning of the system tends to be a positive choice, rather than a criticism.[9]

Moreover, opposition to how the academic system works would appear to be mounted, at least in certain cases, in the name of fundamental institutional values. Thus, students who say that the main function currently performed by higher education is the training of secondary school teachers – scarcely a positive view, since only 1 per cent of respondents thought that this *ought* to be its main role – identified research or, especially, general culture, as their ideal.

This observation extends to the most popular ideal among students: an education 'permitting the individual to act in the modern world and to understand it'. Closely corresponding to one of the privileged themes in current student ideologies, this humanist ideal defines education as culture, and sets it in opposition to the training of specialists or technicians.

Philosophy students selected the ideal of the 'critical spirit' more often than 'humanist training'. This is the most current and also the most traditional way in which philosophy and philosophical training are represented. Given that it is philosophy students more than others who choose this function to describe both the real world of higher education and its ideal role,[10] we may well conclude that adherence to institutional values is greatest when it concerns the most traditional values.[11] Moreover, as a large proportion of students in the so-called scientific disciplines of psychology and sociology also define their ideal as the cultivation of the 'critical spirit', the academic system appears to be able to impose its traditional values on students, whatever the level of their outward opposition [see tables 3.1 and 3.2].

Student background and the academic system

The aims which young people associate with their studies and the extent of their dependence on the university system vary according to the place which each category of student, as distinguished by particular background characteristics, occupies within the system, and indeed within society more broadly.

Table 3.1 Image of major function performed by higher education according to student's field of study (%)

Image of major function	Philosophy (n = 141)	Sociology (n = 109)	Psychology (n = 156)
Critical spirit	11	7	3
General culture	11	14	7
Research	3	3	2
Expert knowledge	26	28	51
Humanist education	7	4	3
Professional training	10	5	3
Teacher training	13	6	10
Selection	19	33	21
Total	100	100	100

Table 3.2 The ideal aims of higher education according to student's field of study (%)

Ideal aim	Philosophy (n = 141)	Sociology (n = 109)	Psychology (n = 156)
Critical spirit	31	25	18
General culture	12	4	4
Research	7	11	13
Expert knowledge	6	5	6
Humanist education	27	38	31
Professional training	13	16	27
Teacher training	4	0	0
Selection	0	1	1
Total	100	100	100

Social class differences Contrary to what we might have expected, today's opposition to the university system does not come from working-class students. Upper-class students are more likely than others to define *professional training* as the aim of higher education. This can be seen by examining the percentages of students from different social backgrounds choosing particular goals and the rank which each goal occupies (see table 3.3).[12] The working classes and the middle classes, on the other hand, display much greater fidelity to the values of the 'critical spirit' and 'general culture'.[13]

The commitment of working-class students to traditional institutional values is proportional to their greater dependence on formal education. The academic system is more successful in imposing on them than on other students the notion that the actual function of higher education is the development of critical thinking among young people.[14] And even when they prefer other images to describe the dominant feature of today's system, they are still more likely than others to choose the transmission of theoretical knowledge.[15]

Now the criticism most frequently levelled at working-class pupils by their teachers in school is a lack of critical spirit and of culture.[16] Bearing this in mind, as well as the fact that the supreme values in the name of which university students are judged involve a particular frame of mind which is above all a social heritage, it is hardly surprising that young people who have not received this heritage should be all the more conscious of the institutional values which sanction it, and that they should be so much more inclined to expect the education system to pass on to them what it implicitly demands of them.

Table 3.3 Ideal aims of higher education by social origin (%)

Image of major function	Working classes[a] (n = 86)	Middle classes[b] (n = 94)	Upper classes[c] (n = 147)
Critical spirit	36	17	22
rank =	I	II	III
General culture	7	13	3
rank =	V	V	VI
Research	5	16	8
rank =	VI	III	IV
Expert knowledge	9	4	4
rank =	IV	VI	V
Humanist education	30	33	34
rank =	II	I	I
Professional training	12	16	24
rank =	III	III	II
Teacher training	1	1	3
rank =	–	–	–
Selection	0	0	2
rank =	–	–	–
Total	100	100	100

[a] Farm-workers, industrial workers, office-workers.
[b] Artisans, shopkeepers, middle managers.
[c] Senior managers, liberal professions.

To upper-class students, more than others, higher education should focus on professional training; but they are also more inclined to nominate the ideal of humanist education. Matching their interest in professional training[17] is a perception that the major function actually performed by the academic system is social selection through qualifications.[18] Far from a working-class protest against biased selection, this attitude expresses the satisfaction of the upper classes with an instrumental higher education which dispenses qualifications that 'permit access to important positions' in society.[19] A preference for professional training is understandable among young people from managerial and professional backgrounds, for how otherwise to conserve and justify social rank except through university qualifications and professional careers? But professional training is not all that these students demand of higher education. Their desire for a broad education to deal with problems in their human context and to transcend the narrowness of the expert betrays a search for symbolic confirmation of their hereditary right to occupy positions of power and prestige.[20]

Table 3.4   The ideal aims of higher education according
to location of university (%)[a]

Ideal aim	Paris	Provinces
Critical spirit	26	33
General culture	8	15
Professional training	22.5	7
Other ideal aims	43.5	45
Total	100	100

[a] Philosophy students (n = 134)

Paris versus the provinces   Residence in Paris versus the provinces contributes
significantly to how university students see the ideal and actual roles
of higher education. The likelihood of sociology students, for example,
nominating the ideal of a 'humanist education' varies as much on this factor
as it does between bourgeois and working-class students.[21] These phenomena
are not unrelated, in fact, as students from lower-status backgrounds are
proportionately more numerous in the provinces [see table 3.4].

It is in the provinces, as we might have expected, that agreement with
traditional institutional values is strongest. Another finding bears out this
more dependent outlook of provincial students on the academic system.
When asked to describe the kinds of teaching practice which they would
prefer, including the roles of different academic staff, provincial students are
very much less likely to question the existing hierarchy of ranks, and this
holds for both sociology and philosophy students [see table 3.5].[22]

Male and female students   Viewed in isolation, some of the findings from our
survey suggest that a group of female university students rejects the traditional
models which govern feminine attitudes in our society, and attaches a
practical purpose to their studies – training for a profession. Among philosophy and psychology students, young women are as likely as young men to
prefer professional training as the goal of higher education; while among
sociology students, they are proportionately three times as likely to nominate
this goal (24%, as against 8%, respectively). Finally, it is only among
females reading philosophy that there is a significant proportion of responses
in favour of teacher training. However, these results may also suggest that
traditional models play a continuing, though hidden, role. For teaching is
traditionally considered to be suited to women; sociology is a discipline
whose professional outcomes are the least certain and the least specific; and

Table 3.5 Preferred teaching staff by university location (%), showing type of teaching staff first nominated

Location	Discipline	Preferred Teaching staff		Total
		Professor	Other staff	
Paris (n = 91)	Philosophy	73.5	26.5	100
	Sociology	64.0	36.0	100
Provinces (n = 155)	Philosophy	97.0	3.0	100
	Sociology	84.0	16.0	100

the attitudes of female sociology students are very similar to those of young women in psychology, a highly feminized discipline and a vocation viewed as feminine.[23]

Moreover, women in philosophy are more inclined than men to choose 'general culture' as the goal of university studies and less likely to select research and the transmission of theoretical knowledge.[24] General culture slips from the third- to the sixth-ranking goal and from 17 per cent of female students in philosophy to only 7 per cent of young men. Women in sociology and psychology are also more likely than men to demand a 'humanist education permitting us to act in the modern world and to understand it'. Thus, here and there, in different guises, those traditional attitudes reappear which Compte thought he had captured definitively: it was to the affective sex, the mediator between humanity and the male sex, that the Supreme Being had entrusted his moral providence.

Young women find higher education too theoretical, and identify with the social definition of their place in the world by seeing their studies as a preparation for roles that have traditionally devolved on them.[25]

II UNIVERSITY STUDENTS AND METHODS
OF TEACHING

Academic teaching is denounced by the new ideologies of education for its unequal relationship and for the passivity which it imposes on students; an academic democracy should be installed in its place, based on interactive methods and small-group work. To some, these demands are part of a wider social revolution, while to others they are simply the utopian dream of a bunch of activists. But in each case it is recognized that they herald the arrival of new social groups in higher education.

Small-group instruction was a particular focus of our survey. Were students who favoured this approach rejecting traditional methods and demanding a complete transformation of the teaching relationship? How important were student background characteristics in influencing attitudes to teaching? If a challenge was being made to the traditional methods of teaching, linked as these are to the kinds of social functions performed by the academic system, did this come from working-class and middle-class students taking issue with an education too closely adapted to the upper classes?

Small-group instruction and the teaching relationship

A preference for teaching in small groups is indeed more pronounced among some categories of students than others, especially young people from working-class backgrounds. But our survey data show that when the nature of the relationship between teacher and student is directly questioned, working-class students prove to be the most individualistic and the most favourable to 'directiveness'.

To fully exploit the data on desired teaching modes, we constructed an 'interactive teaching' index. This compares the number of instructional activities selected by a student which imply some kind of teacher–student interaction or group co-operation with the total number of teaching activities chosen by that student. Interactive or co-operative instruction includes practical work in small groups, with or without a lecturer present; group presentations; discussion during lectures; non-directive debates; and group work from a multicopied text.

The interactive teaching index measures preferences for small-group instruction or 'dialogue' with academic staff.[26] The index proved to be sensitive, first, to how students from different academic disciplines see intellectual work.[27] Philosophy students, for example, turn out to be the most individualistic. Secondly, the index is linked to the living conditions of students. Those who have independent accommodation obtain higher scores than those who are living with their parents, while students who live in university hostels have the highest index scores of all. Social integration in a student milieu thus plays an important role. For example, students living in the provinces obtain higher scores on the interactive teaching index than those living in Paris.[28]

Working-class students, whether they are taking philosophy or sociology, are more likely to favour co-operative teaching approaches than their upper-class counterparts and, in particular, middle-class students.[29]

Women students are also more likely to favour interactive or co-operative

Table 3.6 Interactive teaching scores by social origin (%)

	Low	Medium	High	Total
Working classes[a]	11	48	41	100
Middle classes[b]	30	33	37	100
Upper classes[c]	23	50	27	100

[a] Farm-workers, industrial workers, office-workers.
[b] Artisans, shopkeepers, middle managers.
[c] Senior managers, liberal professions.

Table 3.7 Interactive teaching scores and student activism (%)

Participation	Low	Medium	High	Total
Indifferent, hostile (n = 129)	40	34	26	100
Followers (n = 177)	35	34	31	100
Activists, militants (n = 63)	11	38	51	100

teaching. But the greatest differences are associated (as we might have expected) with student activism. The majority of militants or active participants obtain the highest scores on the interactive teaching index [see table 3.7].

However, to fully understand the meaning of these results, we need to see how students react when the traditional teaching relationship is put directly into question. To explore this dimension, we will focus on views about practical work.[30] In the questionnaire, three types of teacher–student collaboration were specified: presentations by a teacher in front of students, tasks jointly performed by teachers and students, and work done under teacher supervision. To what extent do students want to work collaboratively with their professors, or at any rate with staff responsible for practical work? Should it happen that those students most favourable in general terms to co-operation also tend to reject the type of collaboration involved in practical work – even where this is specifically sanctioned by the system and is not actually prevented by sheer physical constraints – then it could be argued that preference for small-group teaching and 'dialogue' really only reflects

Table 3.8 Preferred teaching relationship in practical work by location of university (%)

Type of practical work	Paris	Provinces
Conducted in front of students	8	13
Conducted in common with students	79	59
Conducted by students under teacher supervision	13	28
Total	100	100

the generalized malaise of students under the traditional academic regime, rather than being a desire to overturn the whole system [see table 3.8].

Even though the majority of students, whatever their background, are in favour of collaborative teaching methods, significant differences occur. For example, provincial students are more likely than those living in Paris to accept 'directiveness' and what might be appropriately called passivity.[31] They hesitate to reduce the distance established by the traditional teaching relationship, and once again reveal more scholastic attitudes and a greater submissiveness to the system.

Similar remarks apply to working-class and middle-class students. Depending on the academic discipline, both are more likely than their upper-class counterparts to prefer work performed by a teacher in front of his students[32] or work performed by the class under the direction of a teacher.[33] Least equipped with an authoritative sense of self-assurance, their awareness of cultural distance inhibits the desire to reduce the distance in teaching.

Differences in views about the instructional relationship in practical work run in the reverse direction to differences over small-group teaching. As a result, we would be justified in concluding that an interest in collaborative instructional approaches does not imply a questioning of the traditional teaching relationship. And, indeed, to the extent that this relationship is brought into question, it is not the newer social groups enrolling in higher education – working-class and middle-class students – who are most inclined to this.

Master and pupil

Under a system of teaching of the traditional type, which may include charismatic elements, the professorial function retains some features of the sacerdotal function with which it was for a long time confused.

Our preparatory interviews, as well as the open-ended question on preferred types of teaching in the questionnaire, revealed two kinds of student expectations regarding the role of today's university teacher. He needs to communicate knowledge, which requires specific skills and clarity of presentation. But, on the other hand, he must have 'personality', and display depth of thought. In short, he must be a master, as well as an initiator, capable of transmitting various ineffable qualities: 'You have to be able to feel the presence of the lecturer.' 'The lecturer ought to make people think . . . like in meditation. . . . Doesn't matter if you can't take notes.' 'I prefer lecturers who can get their ideas across, who can communicate an experience. . . . You have to have the impression that the lecturer actually believes in what he's saying. . . . He has to be in a kind of magnetic state . . . then contact occurs.' 'You need lectures which are really more like conferences, not academic at all.' 'You need magistral lectures . . . given by researchers with a message to get across.' 'A clear and well-organized lecture.' 'We don't need lecturers who just read books to us . . . the personality of the lecturer should stand out.' 'A lecturer with a particular bent of mind . . .'. 'A lecture that's clear and easy to take notes from.'

Views of teaching fall into two extreme categories: initiation into mysteries and infusion of grace, on the one hand, and impersonal communication of a particular body of knowledge, on the other. Between these two poles lies the virtuoso performance, or 'cultivated' finesse.

Students in the main prefer the 'profound' or 'personal' lecture. However, it is striking how often the instrumental demand for an 'indication of the plan' or for the 'possibility of taking notes' occurs, given that this is hardly consistent with the preferred style of lecturing. Many students do, in fact, want a 'clear exposition', which is impersonal and which presents a definite sequence of knowledge. Thus, if one section of the student population inclines towards the researches of the intellectual master, the dominant concern for other students is scholastic effectiveness; or, rather, nearly all students seem to equally and inconsistently share both expectations [see table 3.9].

Female students differ from male students less in their desire for a 'plan', than in a very marked preference for the 'personal lecture' over the impersonal presentation.[34] If one group of male students is interested only in assimilating knowledge, with the lecturer viewed simply as a repository of learning, female students here manifest a desire for personal contact and for domination by the master.

Working-class students choose the 'personal' and the 'brilliant' lecture less often than other groups. They prefer the kind of teaching which, if it enjoys less prestige and has less ambitious aims, is more accessible and more productive [see table 3.10].[35]

Table 3.9   Preferred quality of lectures

Characteristic	Frequency
Scholarly	84
Clear and objective	91
Brilliant	12
Personal	163
Clear, with a plan	25
Brilliant, with a plan	13
Personal, with a plan	52
Total	440

Table 3.10   Preferred quality of lectures by social origin (%)

Preferred quality of lectures	Working classes[a] (n = 97)	Middle classes[b] (n = 95)	Upper classes[c] (n = 172)
Scholarly	27	16	19
Clear and objective	21	23	16
Total	48	39	35
Brilliant	1	2	5
Personal	30	41	40
Total	31	43	45
Other responses	21	18	20
Grand total	100	100	100

[a] Farm-workers, industrial workers, office-workers.
[b] Artisans, shopkeepers, middle managers.
[c] Senior managers, liberal professions.

Similar social patterns in preferred teaching style appear, sometimes more clearly, when students are grouped by the educational level of their fathers, rather than by their father's occupational background. In philosophy, psychology and sociology, preference for the 'scholastic' lecture grows as we move down the scale of educational attainment. Only 17 per cent of students whose fathers obtained the *baccalauréat* want this methodical approach, as compared to 21 per cent with the elementary school certificate and 40 per cent with a junior secondary certificate. Conversely, the weakest support for the 'personal lecture' comes from the group whose fathers have only the junior secondary certificate (37 per cent), as against 49.5 per cent for the elementary school certificate and 55 per cent for children of *baccalauréat*-holders.

Again, among sociology and psychology students, those from culturally disadvantaged backgrounds are less likely to choose the 'personal lecture' than students from cultivated homes (50 per cent, as compared to 61 per cent), and they more often prefer the 'clear and impersonal' lecture (27 per cent, as against 16 per cent).

Thus, whichever method we adopt to group students by their social origins, whether by occupation or by family educational level, it is lower-class and middle-class students who want lectures which enable the student to subsequently retain and assimilate the material covered or which are easy to follow and absorb.

But this desire, at least among working-class students, is not accompanied by a rejection of the profound lecture or the lecture stamped with the seal of passion and personal insight. We are really in the presence of two demands, coexisting in the same individuals.[36] Indeed, if young people from working-class homes less frequently choose the 'personal lecture' without qualification, they more often add the requirement 'indication of plan and ability to take notes'. The result is that if all references to the 'personal lecture' are included, whether accompanied by qualifications or not, there is little to separate the different social classes at all (47, 51 and 52 per cent). It is only when educational level is taken into account that we encounter a clear rejection of the 'personal lecture'. This occurs among those fractions of the middle classes where the father has obtained the junior secondary certificate.

CONCLUSION

Student views regarding the aims and methods of teaching conceal, but at the same time reveal, deeper attitudes. These can be understood in terms of an ideal-typical logic which takes fully into account factors which the actual behaviour of students reflects only confusingly. What meaning young people give to their studies and the particular attitudes which they develop towards teaching must always be seen in terms of their past situation and their likely future, and their place within the university system, as well as within the wider society.

For working-class and middle-class students, the issue is how to acquire the spirit and culture peculiar to higher education, the type of education which symbolizes membership of the elite. For bourgeois students, the task is either to perfect the general education which guarantees their privileges or to obtain qualifications and to enter careers without which they risk losing their status. Young people from working-class or middle-class backgrounds are much more likely to recognize and to share traditional institutional values when they are remote from them, thanks to the culture which they inherit from their families. They will feel the distance which is unmistakably present in the teaching relationship the strongest. But as they are also more dependent on the system, more subordinated to its demands and more sensitive to its influences, they are less likely to question its methods, and they display a scholastic zeal which is at its greatest among middle-class students. Lower-status students look for the support of a group, and hope to establish dialogue with academic staff in order to reduce their malaise, but it is through individualism and submission that middle-class students try to reach their goals. They prefer the most scholastic methods of teaching to the professorial presentation which demonstrates the qualities expected of students while withholding from those who lack them the necessary means of acquiring them.[37]

Young women differ from young men on some attitudes in the same way that working-class students differ from bourgeois students.[38] Their desire for small-group work and for a teaching relationship based on personal domination by the master, their greater acceptance of traditional institutional values, suggest that women continue to submit to, and to prepare themselves for, the roles that have traditionally devolved on them in society.

Alienated by the system and protesting against it, university students yet remain dominated by the ends it pursues and the values it reveres.

APPENDIX 1   IDEAL AIMS AND PERCEIVED IMAGES OF HIGHER EDUCATION AMONG UNIVERSITY STUDENTS

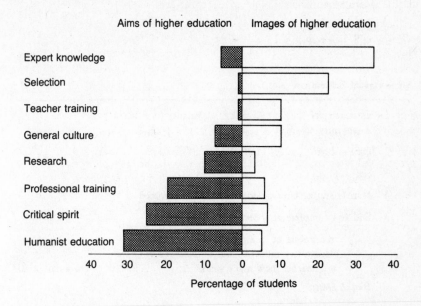

APPENDIX 2   OCCUPATIONAL BACKGROUND BY AGE OF STUDENTS IN PHILOSOPHY, SOCIOLOGY AND PSYCHOLOGY

Occupational background of father	Age of students (%)				
	Below 21	From 21 to 23	Over 23	Total	Relative share[a]
Farm-workers	19	58	23	100	6.3
Industrial workers	24	52	24	100	5.2
Office-workers	44	41	15	100	10.0
Artisans, shopkeepers	38	43	19	100	10.2
Middle managers	45	40	15	100	14.2
Senior managers, liberal professions	38	41	21	100	37.5
Others and missing	28	44	28	100	16.6
Total	36	43	21	100	100 (n = 410)

[a] Numbers in each occupational category expressed as a percentage of all students.

APPENDIX 3   THE QUESTIONNAIRE

Centre de sociologie Européenne
10, rue Monsieur-le-Prince
Paris 6

Sociology of Education

---

1   University of .... Faculty (or School) ....
    Anonymity no ....

2   Date of birth ....

3   Sex ....

4   Marital status: Unmarried – Married – Divorced.

5   Did you complete your secondary education:

    –   in a public or in a private school?
    –   a secondary modern (*cours complémentaire*) or *lycée*?
    –   as a boarder (how many years? ....) or a day-pupil?

6   *Baccalauréat*:

    First part, Series .... Grade ....
    Second part, Series .... Grade ....

7   Did you fail any subjects at the *baccalauréat* exams?

    First part: Yes – No.
    Second part: Yes – No.

8   In what year did you enter the faculty (or school)? ....

9   Have you failed any higher education exams? Yes – No.
    If yes, how many? ....

10 What certificates (or exams) are you preparing for this year? ....
    ....

11 Do you reside:

    –   with your parents?
    –   in a student residential college?
    –   in a hotel?
    –   in private boarding?
    –   in a private room?
    –   in a private flat?
    –   other (specify)?

12 Time usually taken by you to reach the university? ....

13 From which of the sources below do you derive your income?

- scholarship
- salary (studentship, etc.)
- family assistance
- income from work

If the last, what kind of work do you do? ....
....
Average number of hours per week ....

14 What is the occupation of:

Your father? ....
Your mother? ....

15 What is the highest level of qualification obtained by:

Your father? ....
Your mother? ....

16 (1) Among the range of different activities which are used in teaching (lectures, practical work, etc.), which do you think are desirable?

To enable us to compare answers, you will find below a list of the main elements involved in teaching. Each of these elements is designated by a letter or number.

First select from this list the elements that you consider to be essential in teaching, using the relevant symbols to enter these in table 1.

Then complete tables 2 and 3 in the same way, if you wish to identify additional activities.

(You will find an example on the attached sheet.)

Table 1

Participants		Activities	Features
A	F	1	a b
B	G	2	a b
C	H	3	a b c
D	I	4	a b
E		5	a b c d
		6	a b
		7	a b
		8	a b

(2) In the space below, please indicate optionally the reasons for your choice.

Elements of teaching

Participants

A = professor
B = lecturer/demonstrator
C = student instructor
D = technical assistant
E = group leader

F = fewer than 10 students
G = fewer than 25 students
H = between 25 and 50 students
I = more than 50 students

Activities

Characteristics

1 = Exercises, problems, orals, etc.

a = marked
b = not marked

2 = Papers

a = prepared by a student
b = prepared by a small group of students

3 = Use of technical facilities, experiments, analysis of documents, texts, etc.

a = by a teacher before students
b = in common with a teacher
c = under teacher direction

4 = Multicopied texts

a = read and commented upon by the author
b = distributed to students and worked on collectively

5 = Lectures

a = dictated, or delivered in a way enabling notes to be taken
b = clear and objective presentation of facts and theories, without taking an attitude
c = brilliant exposition, in major conference style
d = an at-times 'passionate' presentation, involving personal views or based on in-depth research

6 = Asking questions

a = interrupting a lecture
b = following a presentation

7 = Debate

a = non-directed, based on a topic chosen by all
b = teacher directed, based on a topic chosen by him

8 = Correction of assignments or essays, etc.

a = short indication of what is required

b = complete review, constituting a model

Example of an answer

If you thought it was essential to have lectures dictated by a professor to 40 students who could interrupt with questions, you would mark (in table 1): in the column under 'participants', the letter A (a professor) and the letter H (between 25 and 50 students); in the column under 'activities and features', the number 5 (lectures) and on the same line the letter 'a' (dictated), the number 6 (questions) and the letter 'a' (interrupting the presentation). This would give the following table:

Participants	Activities		Features
(A)	F	1	a b
B	G	2	a b
C	(H)	3	a b c
D	I	4	a b
E		(5)	(a) b c d
		(6)	(a) b
		7	a b
		8	a b

If you thought it was desirable to have, in addition to lectures, the possibility of giving papers followed by a discussion directed by a lecturer/demonstrator, you would use the second table and mark the letters and numbers which identified these elements (in the 'participants' column B designates a lecturer/demonstrator, etc.)

If you thought that these two forms of teaching should be complemented by a third, you would use table 3 to describe this.

17 In your view, are the teaching facilities described below indispensable, useful, not useful (or of little use), or should they be abolished in teaching in the following disciplines?

	Sociology	Philosophy	Psychology
	Essential	Essential	Essential
	Useful	Useful	Useful
	Not useful	Not useful	Not useful
	Abolish	Abolish	Abolish
Maps, graphics			
Tape-recorders			
Films			
Manuals			
Teaching machines			
Photos, transparencies			
Multicopied hand-outs			
Exhibits			
Radio			
Blackboard			
Television			

18   Which of the aspects mentioned below are those which characterize higher education in France today, *according to the experience which you have had in your studies?*

Higher education:

     (a)   initiates and involves students in research;

     (b)   develops a critical spirit;

     (c)   gives an education which allows the individual to act in the modern world and to understand it;

     (d)   gives professional training;

     (e)   gives theoretical knowledge in specific domains of learning;

     (f)   trains teachers for secondary school;

     (g)   imparts general culture;

     (h)   selects students by conferring qualifications which enable them to obtain important positions in society.

Note these aspects below, beginning with what in your eyes is *the most characteristic* and identifying them with the appropriate letter:

Most characteristic aspect ....

Second aspect ....

Third aspect ....

19 In your opinion, which *aim should (or ought to be) essential* to higher education? Answer, using the same system of notation as above.

Principal aspect ....

Second aspect ....

Third aspect ....

20 How many hours of lectures, practical work, etc., per week do you normally have to take?
Total ....

21 How many did you miss during the last week? (Don't count absences due to illness) ....

22 Have you decided on the occupation which you hope to enter on the completion of your studies, or have you still to decide?

23 If you have made up your mind, what occupation have you chosen? ......

24 Do you feel under pressure to abandon your studies before obtaining the qualifications you are aiming at? Yes – No.
If yes, is this:

- for financial reasons;
- because of failure in examinations;
- other reasons
  (please specify ....)?

25 Do you belong to a student working group? Yes – No.
If not, would you like to join one? Yes – No.

26 How would you rate yourself on the scale below regarding your participation in political life?

Militant or active   Follower   Indifferent   Hostile to any participation
participant

27 How would you rate yourself on the scale below regarding your participation in union life?

Militant or active   Follower   Indifferent   Hostile to any participation
participant

Remarks on the questionnaire

Here we wish to clarify a survey technique which avoids the drawbacks of classically framed questions which are often too direct or leading and which yield only stereotyped opinions.

By employing in question 16 the technique of an *à la carte* choice of different teaching activities (the comparison being explicitly made in verbal instructions), all choices and all rejections are made possible without suggesting any one of them directly. A rejection which a student might not dare to express in answer to a direct question can here operate under cover of technical reasons or under the appearance of involuntary omission. Moreover, the necessity of building up teaching activities from their elements makes possible, without actually suggesting it, the choice of new formulas. Thus, e.g., one could have put together from selected elements on the list different formulas for group work; but it would also have been possible to give every good reason for not doing so: 'There was no mention of this . . .'; 'There was not enough space . . .'; etc.

On the other hand, the question brings in a hierarchical construction of different formulas, activities and teachers. It permits a grasp of structures: What activities are expected from what kinds of teachers? What activities are associated (or not associated) with such-and-such other activity?

Do the advantages which this technique offers outweigh its drawbacks? According to students who were asked about it, the apparent complexity of the question was quickly reduced, thanks to the example. The effort demanded no more than what it was actually compared with: choosing from a menu at a restaurant. In addition, it is possible in the analysis of the results to control for this variable: the greater or lesser docility of students (measured, e.g., by reference to the instructions) constituted an index of submission to what could have appeared as a demand from a teacher or as an academic assignment. The very quality of the responses thus gives an indication of attitudes towards teaching and teachers.

NOTES

1 On problems connected with the sample, see chapter 1, introduction.
2 Cf. appendix 3.
3 This last aspect will be covered in a subsequent report.
4 According to Alain, if 'the patience of the workshop' is absent from our classes, this is not only because the teacher likes to talk or because his career depends on his talent for talking, but because education 'aims to distinguish a few individuals from the elite who succeed on their own in mimicking and inventing' (*Propos sur l'éducation*, p. xxxvii).
5 Cf. P. Bourdieu and J.-C. Passeron, *Les Étudiants et leurs études*, Cahiers du Centre de sociologie Européenne, no. 1 (Mouton, Paris and The Hague, 1964).
6 Moreover, in working through the answers, we have only taken into account the first designated function in each of questions 18 and 19 (cf. appendix 3).

7   For a variety of reasons, these results should not be considered as measuring the opinions and attitudes of the whole population of students. However, the answers are similar to those from students in the two control groups to whom the survey was extended: students in English and students in political science.

8   The remarks which follow are based on the cross-tabulation of responses to questions 18 and 19. The observed correlations permit us to verify the negative meaning (i.e., rejection or criticism) or the positive meaning of the selection of a given function as the characteristic feature of education, and to see to what extent the choice of that function tends to be accompanied by the choice either of the same or a similar function or of a very different function as the aim that education *ought ideally* to pursue.

9   Indeed, among students who reported that the most characteristic real feature of education was to dispense general culture, the percentage who made professional training its ideal aim was no greater than the average; whereas the percentage of those who made general culture the ideal (and, to a lesser degree, the percentage of those who favoured the 'critical spirit', which again is a call for a cultural training) was much greater. By comparison, those who favoured professional training as the ideal were even less inclined than others to see this as today's most characteristic function, which they more frequently identified as the transmission of theoretical knowledge.

10   It is only for this function that the percentages vary in the same direction in the two tables (3.1 and 3.2).

11   Whether it concerns different academic disciplines or different social classes, a group of students will adhere all the more to this traditional ideal – the 'critical spirit' – the more they view it as describing the real situation.

12   If we compare the two extreme classes, the difference is statistically significant, $\chi^2 = 5.24$, significant at $p = 0.05$.

13   $\chi^2 = 5.15$, significant at $p = 0.05$. The difference between classes is even greater if we take as an index of the level of social stratification the highest qualification obtained by the student's father. (In this survey, because it concerns teaching attitudes, classification according to this indicator is very often preferable, for it makes the tendencies associated with each occupational group stand out more clearly.) Ten % of students whose fathers held an elementary school certificate opted for vocational training, as against 24% of those whose fathers held the *baccalauréat* or a diploma of higher education.

14   As might be expected, this tendency is particularly strong among philosophy students. Grouped by father's educational level, choice of 'critical spirit' as the most characteristic real function occurs among 11% of C.E.P. holders, 10% of fathers with the junior secondary certificate, and 3% of those with the *baccalauréat*.

15   $\chi^2 = 3.85$, significant at the $p = 0.10$ level.

16   This stereotype appears in particular in the surveys carried out by the Centre de sociologie de l'éducation of Lyon into the attitudes of teachers in the 'reception classes' of *lycées* towards pupils from the *collèges d'enseignement général* (C.E.G.).

17   There is a positive correlation between choice of 'selection by qualifications' as the most characteristic aspect of education and choice of professional training and humanist education as the aim of education.

18 Among philosophy students, 'selection' was designated by the relative majority (22%) of upper-class students, while this choice occupied second rank (17%) among the middle classes and third rank (15%) among the working classes. Among sociology students, the same social pattern is found, where class origin is defined by level of father's qualifications.

19 It is the students who passed their exams with honours and who thus have every chance of qualifying for their degree who most often designate the function of 'selection'.

20 Proof of this is given by the fact that the tendency to favour a 'humanist education' is strongest among students in sociology – a refuge discipline for those whose social status enables them to stay in higher education and an ancillary discipline for students pursuing their main studies in other faculties. (Working classes: 28% with this option ranked second; middle classes: 39% with this option ranked first; upper classes: 45% with this option ranked first.)

21 Percentages for the choice of this function were, respectively, 44% and 32%.

22 Students had to indicate in the table for their responses [appendix 3]: the type of teacher – professor (*professeur*), lecturer (*assistant*), etc. – and the kind of activities which in their eyes constituted the ideal basis of teaching.

23 Differences by sex are very important in this discipline. While the pattern of male choices is very similar to that for male choices in philosophy, female students follow the trend for women in psychology. As these differences are not found between male and female students in other disciplines, we can conclude that they are due to a particular social meaning associated with studying sociology.

24 In philosophy, as in psychology, and for each one of these functions, differences by sex are significant at $p = 0.05$. We have not applied a χ^2 test except when the variations were insufficiently clear to raise doubts about the degree of their significance.

25 Female students more often than male students designate the transmission of theoretical knowledge as the main function presently fulfilled by higher education. In philosophy, the percentages are 31% and 20%, in psychology 57% and 39%, respectively.

26 We can be sure that we have thus measured the same tendencies as those which came to light in participation at the G.T.U. [*groupe du travail universitaire*] by having recorded a positive correlation between the index and attitudes towards student work in groups (question 25).

27 This is why we have examined the influence of background variables within each discipline.

28 In philosophy, 26% of students from the provinces have a high index score, as against 10% from Paris. In previous surveys (cf. Bourdieu and Passeron, *Les Étudiants et leurs études*, p. 37), demands for greater student–teacher contact were also found to occur more frequently in the provinces than in Paris.

29 If we take into account the cultural level of the family, the index scores of the middle socio-cultural stratum are even weaker.

30 Student presentations, which constitute a distinct type of activity in the questionnaire, have been excluded.

31 The results in the table are only for sociology students. The difference is significant at the p = 0.05 level.

32 This is generally the case with middle-class students (12%, as against 5% for upper-class students).

33 Philosophy: working classes, 24%; bourgeois class, 17%. Psychology: working classes, 27%; bourgeois class, 18%.

34 This tendency exists in all disciplines, but it is particularly pronounced, as we might have expected, in philosophy: 22% of female students, as against 35% of male students, favour the 'clear and objective' lecture; 62% of females, against 50% of males, prefer the 'personal' lecture.

35 In contrasting the first two types of lectures with the others and the two extreme social strata, $\chi^2 = 4.08$, significant at p = 0.05 level.

36 The analysis used a technique specifically designed to measure different, and even opposing, tendencies.

37 If the resources which some students use in fact contradict the aims which they say they are pursuing (in conformity with the values of the system), this would at least partly explain the malaise which they and their teachers experience and which some would view as going to the heart of present problems in the teaching situation.

38 This hypothesis receives support from previous surveys.

4

The Users of Lille University Library

Pierre Bourdieu
Monique de Saint Martin

For practical reasons, our study of university students and their use of institutional libraries has been restricted to the users of Lille University Library, implying a more limited range of objectives than would have been possible with access to other survey methods and techniques.[1] How library reading varies in relation to other reading, for example, and how attitudes to the range of institutional libraries (university libraries, libraries of specialized institutes) differ by student background are questions which would have required a sample survey. Having decided to limit the study to measuring user attitudes to the University Library and its services, we also had to forego objective information on student behaviour which could have been gathered only through systematic observation.[2]

The University Library, thanks to its multi-purpose character, lends itself to a variety of uses, and this provides the opportunity to describe the diversity of relationships which students develop towards the facilities which the academic system puts at their disposal. If its specific role is to provide students with instruments of study not otherwise available to them – texts, reference works, catalogues, bibliographical support – the Library also offers itself as a place of study where scholarly activity, the reading of lecture notes or the preparation of assignments can be carried out without resorting to any of the library's specific resources. Obvious and easily recognized, these functions conceal others which are very frequently associated with them, such as using the library as a meeting-place.

There is no better definition of the real function of the University Library than the objective meaning implicated in the use which students make of it.

Asked about what they were doing in the Library on the day of our survey, 38 per cent said they were completing an assignment for which they had used none of the tools supplied by the Library (catalogues, reference works, textbooks); 24.5 per cent said they had consulted reference works; while only 25.5 per cent had used the Library in the way it was specifically designed – to borrow books to read there or at home.[3]

Students in their great majority do nothing at the Library which they cannot do as well or better at home because, by unanimous consent, the Library is an unfavourable site for scholarly reflection. This finding bears out the impression, if any confirmation were needed, that most users of the University Library only appear to be working rather than actually getting anything done. During our pilot survey, some 33 different kinds of activity were observed. Of these, 22 suggested distraction or relaxation, with some students endlessly checking their watches as if they were about to leave, others chatting continually with their neighbours or getting more involved in what their friends were doing than in their own work.[4] University students thus seem to want something from the Library which they cannot find at home, whether this is the real or imaginary encouragement to study induced by the 'atmosphere' of the Library or the psychological gratifications of contact with their peers, known or unknown, or a vague expectation of making these contacts.

Nothing is thus further removed from the rational utilization of all the possibilities offered by the Library than the behaviour of the great majority of students. From the failure to understand the services which specialist library staff provide or the role of the card-index[5] to the type of work carried on while fritting away time chatting or coming and going, everything confirms the fact that students misrecognize the particular function of the Library and more often treat it as a meeting-place or at best a study area. Further confirmation of this comes from the finding that when invited to share their expectations regarding the organization of library services, very few students (12 per cent) want technical improvements to the specific tools of intellectual work supplied by the university library (catalogues, loan service, etc.).

Student attitudes are defined more or less explicitly by reference to an image of work in a library as being seen to be at work, and it is because of this that the will to get some work done (as distinct from merely appearing to work) can lead to refusing to work in the Library just as well as working there from a rational and resolute sense of commitment.

It would be tempting to explain much of this behaviour by pointing to physical conditions, especially poor or inadequate facilities (shortage of study areas, for example). In fact, this would be to make the common assumption that objective conditions directly govern attitudes or actually produce them, so that for a change in attitudes to occur, only a change in the material environment is needed. This illusion of a spontaneous sociology fails to take into account the fact that 'Material conditions can to a large extent aid or inhibit the development of corresponding lines of behaviour, but only if there is a pre-existing tendency, for the way in which conditions will be exploited depends on the nature of the people who are to exploit them.'[6] Indeed, it is very doubtful whether, without some kind of external intervention, university students would be able to develop the skills necessary to benefit, fully and uniformly, from the provision of new facilities, and whether new attitudes can be created simply by abolishing penurious conditions. For material impediments, which weigh unequally on students from different social backgrounds, tend to mask underlying cultural obstacles, concealing them especially from the most vocal of critics. Thus, for example, students complain about the lack of books, but, on the other hand, they are poorly trained in bibliographical searches; their reading is too narrowly limited to recommended texts;[7] and the fact that they are always after the same basic textbooks means that the branch library with multiple copies meets their requirements better than the university library equipped for researchers.

More profoundly, though, what is perhaps most strongly conveyed by student attitudes to the University Library is their whole attitude to intellectual work. What most students refuse, consciously or unconsciously, is the notion of library work as a methodical enterprise. For this requires a deliberate rationalization of time and the application of undivided hours to a continuous task; and this approach is diametrically opposed to the typical way of portraying intellectual work in which reading is ideally done in gulps. Nearly all students questioned during our pilot survey said that they preferred reading at home or in circumstances in which other, non-studious activities could be fitted in – the café, outdoors, a walk, on a bed, at a friend's place.

The romantic image of intellectual work, which reserves reading for 'propitious moments', turns work itself into a form of leisure, and dismisses any apprenticeship in intellectual activity based on exercises carried out in a place specifically set aside for them as boring. 'I don't like the atmosphere of libraries.' 'What puts me off about the Library is the institutional, tedious side. Owning a book makes me feel as if it was written for me. Borrowing a book, I feel that it's not addressed to me.' 'I always have 30 books out to read for the exams, and everyday I borrow another one. I say, "everyday", but it's more like every hour! I tell myself I have to read that, then I take the book, read three or four pages, then, at night, another book catches my eye and I take out yet another one.'

These cultural obstacles weigh so heavily on students because they are poorly trained for the rational exploitation of the Library. Thus young people who have spent several years in higher education can still prove to be incapable of using the Library in the way it was specifically intended. 'I quite often go to the University Library to do translations, to use *Harraps*, or for various other things, but I have never borrowed a single book. I don't even know how the system works, the card-index, all that, I have never used it' (female student; father, a middle-level manager; six years at university). In fact, the techniques of bibliographical search are never explicitly taught, in however rudimentary a way.[8]

Significantly, students are able to distance themselves much more from the typical attitude when they are better equipped in terms of methods and techniques of academic work and more capable of integrating library work into a methodical enterprise. Thus 35 per cent of holders of secondary teaching scholarships came to consult the catalogue or to borrow books as against 27 per cent of general scholarship-holders and only 24 per cent of private students. Similarly, more holders of secondary teaching scholarships than private students see the Library exclusively as a place of work, and not as a meeting-place as well as a place of work.[9] Thus, everything happens as if the absence of methodical instruction in the techniques of intellectual work facilitates the law of natural selection coming into play. Only those students who are better armed scholastically are capable of finding in themselves the resources which the institution should provide for all.

* * *

Thus the activities in which students engage most frequently tend to come together in defining the real meaning of work in a university library, and this establishes the framework within which the subjective and the objective significance of individual behaviour is in turn defined, even if the very ambiguity of their relationship with the library implies that students cannot categorically declare the real meaning of their own conduct.

In this context it is remarkable that indirect survey questions should have been able to bring out underlying relationships between student attitudes to seriousness of intellectual work, skills in using library services, or the meanings conferred by students, subjectively or objectively, on work in a library and background characteristics such as number of years at university, sex and occupational category.

For newcomers – preliminary-year students – work in the University Library is one of the surest and easiest ways of achieving the image of the student. Moreover, while in some respects it may restore the atmosphere of compulsory, supervised study in secondary school, the University Library is also the place to encounter what is most specifically and notoriously 'student'. So it is understandable that preliminary-year students should be the main users. The fact that undergraduates, preparing for their *licence*, use Institute libraries as an alternative, is not enough to explain why preliminary-year students, who represent only 30.6 per cent of all arts faculty numbers, should make up 45 per cent of all library-users.

Ambivalent attitudes towards the University Library are particularly marked among female students. Knowing that they are more likely than male students to report working regularly, and that, living more often with their families, they are more strongly attached to the idea of working at home, we might have expected them to be less well represented among users of the University Library. Should we then attribute to a superior academic zeal the fact that, on the contrary, they are more highly represented?[10] In fact, they are more likely to admit that they go to the Library out of a desire to feel enclosed by the surroundings and so to feel 'stimulated in their work', while meeting fellow students at the same time. The Library is a 'place to work where you don't feel isolated'; it offers the satisfactions of studious activity and distracting social contact. 'I like the spectacle of people coming and going'; 'I don't like going there on my own because I get bored to death.' Male students tend to construct a more realistic and less ambivalent picture of the Library. From a menu of alternative images, they often choose the 'railway station', as representing a place of transit and of meetings. But young women reject this analogy, and describe the library as a 'beehive' – a place of intense collective activity in which scholarly zeal and the expectation of meeting friends are merged. They also couple two antithetical images more frequently – 'monastery' and 'railway station', 'beehive' and 'waiting-room' – and through this attempted reconciliation of contraries betray the ambivalent function which the University Library really performs for them.[11] They can thus enjoy working in a noisy atmosphere, and blame the noise for not getting much work done; the Library is for work, but at the same time for meeting friends. Again, by comparison with male students, their ideal image of the Library gravitates towards the beehive or the lecture theatre, while males prefer the monastery. A desire for integration is revealed by these attitudes, as well as by other indicators. Girls more often say that they like to sit close to their friends or try to find out what their neighbours are doing or that they frequently break off their work to talk.

Perhaps these contradictions in attitude should be understood as a response to the 'mixed pressures' experienced by young women caught between the traditional definition of women's role and the situation of female students at university. Young women who come from well-to-do families can view their entry to university in terms of social benefits, without being unaware that their current activity is preparing them in name only for a future which will deny their training.[12] Indeed, female students can respond to contradictory expectations from family, male friends and, in fact, the whole university situation with behaviour which differs from male patterns in two divergent directions. Conformity to the most traditional models of feminine conduct offers them adaptation in the form of academic zeal and docility, evident, for example, in the greater likelihood that they, not their male colleagues, will read recommended texts. But there is still a kind of unconscious fidelity to the most traditional social expectations, which leads them more often than young men – who are better integrated in a badly integrated milieu – to look consciously or unconsciously for meetings and contacts.

Library work authorizes an apparent reconciliation of contraries through a kind of double-game played out with itself. It provides female students – especially those from the most privileged backgrounds – with a way of expressing their ambivalent relationship with their situation, and it is owing to this that their behaviour more completely betrays an attitude found to different degrees among most users of the Library. How can we explain the fact that working-class students – whom we know buy fewer books, have less comfortable accommodation, and are more assiduous at university – frequent the University Library somewhat less often than other students, if we do not admit that, being more conscious of the fictive character of a certain style of library use, they more often choose to work at home? Their attitude, characterized by much greater seriousness of purpose, is formed with reference to the objective definition of the Library as a place in which the impression of work is given – a definition which is more evident to them, and which they express more freely in interviews.[13] It is because of this that they display a greater tendency than other students to absent themselves from the Library. One proof of this is the fact that, with the approach of exams, when the call to be serious is greater than usual, their presence among library-users is even more sparse than during the course of the year.[14] Moreover, there are other signs that when in the Library they work with more seriousness. While, by contrast with upper-class students, they sit closer to their friends, they speak less frequently to them, doubtless because they are less worried about 'making friends'.[15] In short, students are more likely to make the Library a place where the impression of work is given when they come from a more privileged social background.

* * *

'My work isn't unpleasant, it's not an imposition; I could just about say that all the work I do is leisure.' 'For me, there's no such thing as a time for work, a time for leisure; there's just a time of inactivity, with things falling into place.' 'Throughout the year, for me at any rate, work is a kind of leisure, and leisure a kind of work; in short, they overlap.'

For the dilettante, all means will do to break down the boundaries between leisure and work. Just as he can convince himself that certain leisure activities belong to the business of cultural training, so by working in the Library or in the café he can claim the justifications of work done without giving up the satisfactions of leisure.

APPENDIX 1   CHARACTERISTICS OF THE SAMPLE

Father's occupation	Preliminary year[a]	Arts licence	Science	Law	Medicine Pharmacy	Grandes écoles
Farm-workers (n = 48)	10	17	13	5	–	3
Industrial workers (n = 87)	36	30	17	2	–	2
Domestic workers (n = 41)	10	21	6	2	1	1
Office-workers (n = 96)	30	40	19	3	2	2
Artisans, shopkeepers (n = 153)	53	58	30	6	1	5
Middle managers (n = 145)	59	52	26	5	2	1
Senior managers (n = 244)	75	104	44	9	11	1
Others (private income, retired) (n = 66)	13	27	21	3	1	1
Total (n = 880)	286	349	176	35	18	16

[a] Arts Faculty

APPENDIX 2   THE QUESTIONNAIRE

Centre de sociologie Européenne
10, rue Monsieur-le-Prince
Paris 6

Date...

Sociology of Education

1   Hour of arrival .... Hour of departure ....

2   Sex ....

3   Date of birth ....

4   Father's occupation ....
    (Please be as precise as possible: don't say 'teacher', but 'primary school
    teacher' or 'secondary school teacher'; don't say 'worker', but 'semi-skilled
    worker' or 'skilled worker, grade 1').

5   Faculty (or School) ....

6   In what type of school did you do most of your studies? public – private
    Were you: a boarder – a day-pupil?

7   Examinations taken this year:
    ....
    ....
    ....

8   Number of years in higher education (including the present one) ....

9   Place of residence during academic term ....

10   Do you reside:

    – with your parents?
    – in a private room (alone, with two people, with several)?
    – in private boarding?
    – on university premises (residential college or union)?
    – in a hotel?
    – other (specify) ....

11   Are you:

    – a private student?
    – a scholarship-holder?
    – a studentship-holder?

    Are you presently employed:

    – in education? (Specify.)
    – outside education? (Specify.)

12 Approximately how many hours each week do you spend in the University Library? ....

13 What did you do today in the University Library? (Please be as precise as possible.)

....

....

....

14 If you came to borrow a book or to consult one at the Library, was it:

- because a lecturer recommended it?
- because it was listed in a bibliography?
- because a friend spoke to you about it?
- because someone else recommended it to you? (please specify who) . . .
- for other reasons? (Please specify.)

15 As a rule, do you work in an uninterrupted fashion? Yes – No.

If not, do you stop from time to time to:

- daydream?
- speak to your neighbours?
- go for a cigarette, alone or in a group?
- go to a café, alone or in a group?
- for some other reason? (Please specify.)

16 Where do you most often work? (Number in order of importance.):

- at home?
- in a café?
- in the University Library?
- in other libraries? (Please specify.)
- other places? (Please specify.)

17 Do you prefer to sit with your friends? Yes – No.

18 Has the University Library enabled you to make friends with other people this year? Yes – No.

If yes, were these people:

- from the same course?
- from the same faculty?
- from other faculties? (Specify.)

19 Do you try to find out what your neighbours are doing? Yes – No.

If yes, do you try to find out:

- their level of studies?
- their course?
- other? (Please specify.)

20 Do you have a preferred spot in the Library? Yes – No.

If yes, mark the spot with a cross on the plan of the Library below:

Semicircle

Left

Right

If possible, say why ....
....
....

21 Of the following different images, which is the one which most approaches
what the University Library is, in fact, for you?

   – church
   – waiting-room
   – beehive
   – railway station
   – lecture room
   – monastery
   – other images (please specify) ....

Please say why: ....

22 Of the following different images, which one most closely describes the way
the University Library *ought to be*?

   – church
   – waiting-room
   – beehive
   – railway station
   – lecture room
   – monastery
   – other images (please specify) ....

Please say why: ....
....
....

23 What does the Library mean to you, and what do you expect of it?
....
....
....
....

24 Please note below any free observations or wishes you might have with
    respect to the Library?

    . . . .

    . . . .

NOTES

1 The sample comprised 880 students who entered the Library at least once
   between Monday, 16 March, and Saturday, 21 March, 1964. The question-
   naires were distributed at the entrance to the Library by students from the
   sociology group in the Faculty of Arts at Lille, who encouraged their comrades
   to answer them (once only, when they first entered the library). In order to
   verify the results obtained by this survey and to examine the extent to which
   the use of the Library varies according to time of year and proximity of
   examinations, a second very brief questionnaire was administered on 21 May,
   and the 255 responses were analysed separately. We wish to thank Miss A.
   Bruchet, Librarian of the Lille University Library, who permitted us to conduct this survey, and Messrs R. Beghinet and J.-F. Lacascade who carried out
   preparatory observations and organized the pilot study and main survey.

2 Preceding the survey, systematic observation of the behaviour of students in
   the University Library was able to provide only general indications; to link up
   various attitudes with the social characteristics of individuals required us to
   resort to the questionnaire.

3 Given the availability of the loan service, which permits students to come and
   borrow books without entering the Library, the actual proportion of students
   who come to borrow works in order to read them at home is surely greater than
   what the present survey reveals; students who came simply to borrow a book
   without having to search the catalogue did not complete the questionnaire,
   which was distributed at the entrance to the reading room.

4 Many behaviours express the same dilettantism, real or affected: references are
   noted on a matchbox or on the back of an envelope; monumental piles of books
   are returned without having been opened; and so on.

5 Students reject working through a librarian, rarely asking for assistance. 'It is
   very difficult', a librarian says; 'there is a door to go through, they don't know,
   they dare not.'

6 William I. Thomas and Florian Znaniecki, *The Polish Peasant in Europe and
   America*, 2nd edn (New York, Dover, 1958), p. 13.

7 Among users of the loan service, 59% were obeying strictly academic orders,
   whether the work had been explicitly advised by a lecturer or had figured in a
   bibliography handed out by one; only 11% had been advised by a friend.

8 The sheet handed to students at enrolment time in October provides a good
   general guide to the operation of the Library, but it does not constitute an
   initiation into bibliographical techniques. Indeed, for students to know how to

use the system, it is not enough to give them a description of it; it is also necessary to induct them into the techniques of using these instruments.

9 The few law students who frequent the University Library (which is located very close to the Faculty of Arts) have to leave the space of their habitual activity to do this, and it is not surprising to observe that most of them came to borrow books.

10 Young women represent 70% of Library-users coming from the Faculty of Arts, while for the same academic year they represent only 60% of all students enrolled in this Faculty.

11 Invited to give their observations on the subject of the Library, 24% of female students reported expecting to be able to work and at the same time to meet other students, as against only 12% of males. Among young women, 56% adopted as the ideal image the beehive or the lecture room, as against 37% of men, who, conversely, chose the image of the monastery relatively more often (33%, as against 18%). On the other hand, if 29% of male students compared to 13% of females saw in the railway station the image closest to the library in its present form, 10% of young women cited combinations of disparate images evoking at one and the same time a place of work and a meeting-place, something scarcely ever found among male students.

12 Young women from the working classes are clearly distinguished from female students in general by more studious and unequivocal attitudes. In addition, they more often use the Library according to its specific function, locating the most undisturbed areas to work in, away from passages and meeting-places and close to reference books.

13 'It is absolutely impossible to concentrate, to read in a library' (student from an office-worker's background). 'The University Library? No, I don't like it, you can't work there with any conviction. – For my part, when I work I don't like to be disturbed' (student from farmer's background). 'The University Library? No one works there; they just give the impression of working. – As for me, I prefer to work at home' (industrial worker's background).

14 While working-class students represent 23% of students in the Arts Faculty at Lille, they represent only 15% of Arts students who frequent the University Library in the 'normal period' and less than 12% of those who frequent it at the time of exams.

15 We have seen that female students from working-class backgrounds have a different attitude to other female students.

Index